Vocabulary

SIMPLIFIED

STRATEGIES FOR BUILDING YOUR COLLEGE VOCABULARY

SECOND EDITION

VOCABULARY FOR COLLEGE AND WORKPLACE SUCCESS

☆

CONTEXT CLUES

☆

WORD PARTS: ROOTS, PREFIXES, SUFFIXES

☆

VOCABULARY FOR THE 21st CENTURY

☆

WORD MENUS

KATHLEEN T. McWHORTER

Niagara County Community College

PEARSON
Longman

New York   San Francisco   Boston
London   Toronto   Sydney   Tokyo   Singapore   Madrid
Mexico City   Munich   Paris   Cape Town   Hong Kong   Montreal

Senior Acquisitions Editor: Susan Kunchandy
Development Editor: Marion B. Castellucci
Senior Marketing Manager: Melanie Craig
Senior Supplements Editor: Donna Campion
Managing Editor: Bob Ginsberg
Production Manager: Joseph Vella
Project Coordination, Text Design, and Electronic Page Makeup: Thompson Steele, Inc.
Photo Research: Vivette Porges
Cover Designer/Manager: John Callahan
Senior Manufacturing Buyer: Alfred C. Dorsey
Printer and Binder: Courier Corp.–Kendallville
Cover Printer: The Lehigh Press

For permission to use copyrighted material, grateful acknowledgment is made to the copyright holders on p. 147, which are hereby made part of this copyright page.

Library of Congress Cataloging-in-Publication Data:
McWhorter, Kathleen T.
    Vocabulary simplified : strategies for building your college vocabulary / Kathleen T. McWhorter.—2nd ed.
        p. cm.
    ISBN 0-321-14256-X (student ed.) — ISBN 0-321-14258-6 (annotated instructor's ed.)
    1. Vocabulary—Problems, exercises, etc. 2. Universities and colleges—Curricula—Terminology—Problems, exercises, etc.
3. Learning and scholarship—Terminology—Problems, exercises, etc. I. Title.
PE1449.M398 2006
428.1--dc22
                                                                                                2005004758

Please visit our Web site at http://www.ablongman.com

ISBN 0-321-14256-X (Student Edition)
ISBN 0-321-14258-6 (Annotated Instructor's Edition)

1 2 3 4 5 6 7 8 9 10—CRK—08 07 06 05

CONTENTS

Strong vocabulary skills—knowledge about word meanings—are essential for success in college and in the workplace. They are the keys to comprehension and effective self-expression. *Vocabulary Simplified: Strategies for Building Your College Vocabulary* is a brief worktext that contains instruction and extensive practice exercises.

Content Overview

- **Part One, The Whys and Hows of Improving Your Vocabulary,** explains why vocabulary is important, reviews basic dictionary usage skills, discusses the uses of a thesaurus, and presents strategies for learning new words.
- **Part Two, Using Context to Figure Out Words,** teaches students to use context clues to figure out the meanings of unknown words. Five clues are introduced: synonyms, definitions, examples, contrast, and general sense of the passage.
- **Part Three, Using Word Parts to Expand Your Vocabulary,** introduces word parts as a means of vocabulary expansion.
- **Part Four, Vocabulary for the Twenty-first Century,** introduces interesting features of language that are important as language evolves, including foreign words and phrases, euphemisms, doublespeak, neologisms, and analogies.
- **Part Five, A Weekly Menu of New Words,** offers word lists arranged by academic discipline. The lists contain high-utility words that introduce students to each discipline and provide a working vocabulary in each field.

Each part of the book contains numerous exercises designed to guide students in learning the skills taught in each section. Varied exercise formats maintain student interest and require different types of thinking skills.

Special Features

- **Applying and Integrating What You Have Learned:** Exercises are designed to help students apply, integrate, and transfer their learning to academic situations. Excerpts from college textbooks provide relevant, realistic practice materials.
- **Learn More About . . . Web site references:** This feature refers students to Web sites to obtain further information or practice on the skills presented in the chapter.
- **Exploring Language:** These boxes are designed to provoke students' interest in language and introduce them to unique features of language. Topics include new meanings for old words, eponyms, acronyms, and ghost words.

Changes to the Second Edition

This revision is centered on making the book more accessible to students and increasing the number of exercises in Part Three. New features include:

- Addition of visuals, including photographs, cartoons, and word puzzles to add interest and motivate students.

- Inclusion of additional Web site links to provide students with additional resources for word study and research. Web sites have been included for each academic discipline listed in Part Five, as well.
- Approximately 100 additional exercise items have been added to Part Three.
- Part Three now includes paragraph-based prefix, root, and suffix exercises, allowing the students to see the application of word-part study using excerpts from college textbooks.
- A new appendix organizes the prefixes, roots, and suffixes taught throughout Part Three into three alphabetical tables for easy student reference.
- The Answer Key has been deleted from the student text.

The Teaching and Learning Package

Longman is pleased to offer a variety of support materials to help make teaching reading easier on teachers and to help students excel in their coursework. Many of our student supplements are available free or at a greatly reduced price when packaged with a Longman reading or study skills textbook. Contact your local Longman sales representative for more information on pricing and how to create a package.

Support Materials For Reading and Study Skills Instructors

Annotated Instructor's Edition. The annotated instructor's edition is identical to the student text but it includes answers to questions and exercises printed directly on the page (Instructor / ISBN 0-321-14258-6).

Printed Test Bank for Developmental Reading. Offers more than 3,000 questions in all areas of reading, including vocabulary, main idea, supporting details, patterns of organization, critical thinking, analytical reasoning, inference, point of view, visual aides, and textbook reading (Instructor / ISBN: 0-321-08596-5). (An electronic version is also available. See following section.)

Electronic Test Bank for Developmental Reading. Offers more than 3,000 questions in all areas of reading, including vocabulary, main idea, supporting details, patterns of organization, critical thinking, analytical reasoning, inference, point of view, visual aides, and textbook reading. Instructors simply choose questions, then print out the completed test for distribution OR offer the test online (Instructor / CD ISBN: 0-321-08179-X).

The Longman Instructor's Planner. This planner includes weekly and monthly calendars, student attendance and grading rosters, space for contact information, Web references, an almanac, and blank pages for notes (Instructor / ISBN: 0-321-09247-3).

For Students

Vocabulary Skills Study Cards. Colorful, affordable, and packed with useful information, Longman's Vocabulary Study Card is a concise, eight-page reference guide to developing key vocabulary skills, such as learning to recognize context clues, reading a dictionary entry, and recognizing key root words, suffixes, and prefixes. Laminated for durability, students can keep this Study Card for years to come and pull it out whenever they need a quick review (Student / ISBN: 0-321-31802-1).

Reading Skills Study Card.   Colorful, affordable, and packed with useful information, Longman's Reading Skills Study Card is a concise, eight-page reference guide to help students develop basic reading skills, such as concept skills, structural skills, language skills, and reasoning skills. Laminated for durability, students can keep this Study Card for years to come and pull it out whenever they need a quick review (Student / ISBN: 0-321-33833-2).

The Longman Textbook Reader, Revised Edition.   Offers five complete chapters from our textbooks: computer science, biology, psychology, communications, and business. Each chapter includes additional comprehension quizzes, critical thinking questions, and group activities (with answers Student / ISBN: 0-321-11895-2 or without answers Student / ISBN: 0-321-12223-2).

The Longman Reader's Portfolio and Student Planner.   This unique supplement provides students with a space to plan, think about, and present their work. The portfolio includes a diagnostic area (including a learning style questionnaire), a working area (including calendars, vocabulary logs, reading response sheets, book club tips, and other valuable materials), and a display area (including a progress chart, a final table of contents, and a final assessment), as well as a daily planner for students including daily, weekly, and monthly calendars (Student / ISBN: 0-321-29610-9).

The Longman Reader's Journal, by Kathleen McWhorter.   The first journal for readers, The Longman Reader's Journal offers a place for students to record their reactions to and questions about any reading (Student / ISBN: 0-321-08843-3).

10 Practices of Highly Effective Students.   This study skills supplement includes topics such as time management, test taking, reading critically, stress, and motivation (Student / ISBN: 0-205-30769-8).

Newsweek Discount Subscription Coupon (12 weeks).   *Newsweek* gets students reading, writing, and thinking about what's going on in the world around them. The price of the subscription is added to the cost of the book. Instructors receive weekly lesson plans, quizzes, and curriculum guides as well as a complimentary *Newsweek* subscription. The price of the subscription is 59 cents per issue (a total of $7.08 for the subscription). *Package item only* (Student / ISBN: 0-321-08895-6).

Interactive Guide to *Newsweek.*   Available with the 12-week subscription to *Newsweek,* this guide serves as a workbook for students who are using the magazine (Student / ISBN: 0-321-05528-4).

Penguin Discount Novel Program.   In cooperation with Penguin Putnam, Inc., Longman is proud to offer a variety of Penguin paperbacks at a significant discount when packaged with any Longman title. Excellent additions to any developmental reading course, Penguin titles give students the opportunity to explore contemporary and classical fiction and drama. The available titles include works by authors as diverse as Toni Morrison, Julia Alvarez, Mary Shelley, and Shakespeare. To review the complete list of titles available, visit the Longman-Penguin-Putnam Web site: http://www.ablongman.com/penguin.

The New American Webster Handy College Dictionary.   This paperback reference text has more than 100,000 entries (Student / ISBN: 0-451-18166-2).

Merriam-Webster Collegiate Dictionary.   This hardcover comprehensive dictionary is available at a significant discount when packaged with any Longman text (Student / ISBN: 0-321-10494-3).

Multimedia Offerings

Interested in incorporating online materials into your course? Longman is happy to help. Our regional technology specialists provide training on all of our multimedia offerings.

MySkillsLab 2.0 (www.myskillslab.com).   This exciting new Web site houses all the media tools any developmental English student will need to improve their reading, writing, and study skills, and all in one easy to use place. Resources for reading and study skills include:

- Reading Roadtrip 4.0 Web site
- Longman Vocabulary Web site
- Longman Study Skills Web site
- Research Navigator

MySkillsLab 2.0 is available in the following formats: Web site, CourseCompass, WebCT, and Blackboard.

Reading Road Trip 4.0 Plus Web site (www.ablongman.com/readingroadtrip). The best-selling reading site available, Reading Road Trip takes students on a tour of 16 cities and landmarks throughout the United States, with each of the 16 modules corresponding to a reading or study skill. The topics include main idea, vocabulary, understanding patterns of organization, thinking critically, reading rate, notetaking and highlighting, graphics and visual aids, and more. Students can begin their trip by taking a brand-new diagnostics test that provides immediate feedback, guiding them to specific modules for additional help with reading skills. The all-new Reading Road Trip 4.0 PLUS will include:

- **Longman Vocabulary Web site.** This site features hundreds of exercises in ten topic areas to strengthen vocabulary skills. Students will also benefit from "100 Words That All High School Graduates Should Know," a useful resource that provides definitions for each of the words on this list, vocabulary flashcards and audio clips to help facilitate pronunciation skills.

- **Longman Study Skills Web site.** This site offers hundreds of review strategies for college success, time and stress management skills, study strategies, and more. Students can take a variety of assessment tests to learn about their organizational skills and learning styles, with follow-up quizzes to reinforce the strategies they have learned.

- **Research Navigator.** In addition to providing valuable help to any college student on how to conduct high-quality online research and to document it properly, Research Navigator provides access to thousands of academic journals and periodicals (including the NY Times Archive), allowing reading students to practice with authentic readings from college level primary sources.

Reading Road Trip 4.0 PLUS with *CourseCompass*.   Offers all the features of Reading Road Trip 4.0 Plus with course management features—including a grade book to record student progress automatically as they progress through the program and an electronic test bank of over 3,000 questions organized by grade level.

The Longman Vocabulary Web site (http://www.ablongman.com/vocabulary). This unique Web site features hundreds of exercises in ten topic areas to strengthen vocabulary skills. Students will also benefit from "100 Words That All High School Graduates Should Know," a useful resource that provides definitions for each of the words on this list, vocabulary flashcards, and audio clips to help facilitate pronunciation skills (open access).

Longman Study Skills Web site (http://www.ablongman.com/studyskills). This site offers hundreds of review strategies for college success, time and stress management skills, study strategies, and more. Students can take a variety of assessment tests to learn about their organizational skills and learning styles, with follow-up quizzes to reinforce the strategies they have learned (*open access*).

Acknowledgments

The editorial staff of Longman Publishers deserves a special recognition and thanks for the guidance, support, and direction they have provided. In particular I wish to thank Marion Castellucci, my development editor, for her valuable advice and assistance, and Susan Kunchandy, senior acquisitions editor, for her creative ideas and enthusiastic support of the revision of this book. Thanks also to the following reviewers for their suggestions:

Sydney Bartman, Mt. San Antonio College; Diane Beecher, Lake Superior College; Helen R. Carr, San Antonio College; Judi Keen, Sacramento City College; Natalie Miller, Joliet Junior College; Susan Miller, Mesa Community College; Susan Nnaji, Prairie View A & M University; Lisa M. Tittle, Harford Community College; and Kim Zernechel, Minneapolis Community and Technical College.

KATHLEEN T. MCWHORTER

PART ONE

The Whys and Hows of Improving Your Vocabulary

SECTION A ## Your Vocabulary: What Your Professors and Employers Know About You

Boy meets girl. Teacher meets student. Employer meets job applicant. Then what happens?

When people meet for the first time, they size each other up and form first impressions. New acquaintances may size you up by how you look—your clothing, hairstyle, shoes, jewelry, and so forth. They may also size you up by what you say and how you say it. People may notice an accent, the use of slang, the loudness or softness or pitch of your voice, and so forth. They also notice your vocabulary. Every time you begin speaking or as soon as someone reads a sentence you have written, you are revealing something about yourself:

- **You may reveal many personal characteristics.** You may reveal that you are a native or non-native speaker of the language, for example. You may reveal where you live or grew up, based on your accent. Your use of slang may suggest what reference group or age group you belong to. Your use of technical words may reveal your occupation. (Don't physicians often tell you what's wrong with you in language you can't understand? Can't you always tell who is a computer techie as soon as the conversation turns to computers?) Your language, and specifically your vocabulary, may reveal your level of education, too. Professors and employers often can easily pick out those who are college educated from among the individuals in a group. College graduates often speak and write differently, perhaps because they think differently as well.

- **Your vocabulary also reveals whether accurate and clear expression is important to you.** If you usually lack the words to express an idea, you are revealing that effective communication is not a priority. Both in the classroom and in most careers, communication is essential. If you show no interest in communicating effectively, your professor may think you are not a serious student, and an employer may not be interested in hiring you.

- **By observing whether you are speaking and writing in the language of the subject matter you are studying, your professors can assess how interested and involved you are with a course.** If, in a biology class, you are still calling amoebas "those little things swimming around" and, in a chemistry class, you are still calling a beaker a "glass," you are revealing lack of interest in and seriousness about the course.

- **By listening to whether you can describe your prior employment experiences clearly without struggling for words, an employer can learn whether you can focus and organize information.** You also reveal, however, whether you have the words readily at your command to communicate what you know about your job history.

- **Most importantly, through your speaking or writing you reveal your thinking.** It is through language that you share information, express your ideas and feelings, solve problems, and present arguments. Your vocabulary—individual words that you know and use—are the building blocks of language. In both speech and writing, you string them together to express meaning.

So, you can see that vocabulary is important, and probably more revealing than you thought.

SECTION B Vocabulary and College Success

Think about the following questions:

- Why do professors expect you to answer questions in class?
- Why do professors assign papers and give essay exams?
- Why might a professor require you to make a speech or participate in a class discussion?

Let's be practical. There's more to getting good grades than just studying hard. Grades in college depend on tests and exams, papers, oral reports, lab reports, and class participation. Each is a form of self-expression. You not only have to learn the material being tested or reported, you have to demonstrate that you have learned it, either through speech or writing. If you completely understand the theory of cognitive dissonance in psychology, for example, but cannot explain it clearly in your own words on an essay exam, what kind of grade can you expect?

SECTION C Vocabulary and Workplace Success

Question: What do corporations look for in prospective employees?

Answer: The DeVry Institute of Technology conducted a survey to find out which skills and aptitudes corporations value most highly.[1] Of the top ten employee capabilities listed, can you guess what skill was ranked first? Excellent verbal and written skills were the most highly rated. Critical thinking ranked fifth; creative thinking ranked sixth. Both verbal and written skills depend in part on vocabulary, as does critical and creative thinking.

Can you imagine engineers, although technically competent, being unable to explain what they are working on, being unable to describe their role in a project, and being unable to relate their tasks to what others are doing? This lack of communication skills is a problem often cited by employers of engineers.[2] Many employers in a variety of fields report similar problems. Writing in the "Job Market" column that appears regularly in the *New York Times*, Sabra Chartrand reports that even in technical fields, communication skills are highly valued.[3]

Here are two research findings that point to the connection between a strong vocabulary and success in the workplace:

- A study conducted by the U.S. Department of Education concludes that literacy level, which includes knowledge of word meaning, is positively associated with higher annual earnings.[4] In other words, those with stronger literacy skills earned higher salaries.
- A study conducted by the Johnson O'Connor Research Foundation reports that successful executives have better vocabularies than nonexecutives of the same age group.[5]

To get and keep a good job, then, you will need excellent vocabulary skills.

SECTION D Dictionaries: Worthwhile Investments

Item	Estimated Cost
Large pizza (cheese and pepperoni)	$9.00
American Heritage Dictionary (paperback)	5.99
The New American Roget's College Thesaurus in Dictionary Form (paperback)	5.99

Now, which is the best investment? Certainly not the pizza!

To improve your vocabulary, you need the right tools. As you can see, both a paperback dictionary and a paperback thesaurus are great investments. Every college student should own a paperback dictionary, and many students find a thesaurus to be a worthwhile investment as well. In this section, you will learn how to use each to improve your vocabulary. You will also learn about another useful resource, a subject area dictionary.

A Dictionary: Which One to Buy?

Collegiate Dictionaries   You should have at least one dictionary, and it should be a collegiate dictionary or the equivalent. Other dictionaries, such as student dictionaries and pocket dictionaries, are not as useful, since they are written for different audiences (high school students or office personnel, for example), and may not contain as many of the words or meanings you will need. A collegiate dictionary is written with college students in mind. Collegiate dictionaries are available in either hardback or paperback. Desk versions (hardback) contain many more words than do paperback versions and list many more meanings for most words.

The following are the most popular collegiate dictionaries:

New American Webster Handy College Dictionary

American Heritage Dictionary of the English Language

The Random House Dictionary of the English Language

Webster's New World Dictionary of the American Language

Merriam-Webster's Collegiate Dictionary

Online Dictionaries Many different types of dictionaries are available on the World Wide Web. Two of the most widely used English printed dictionaries, those by Merriam-Webster and American Heritage, have Internet versions. Both of these sites (http://www.m-w.com/ and http://www.yourdictionary.com/index.shtml) feature an audio component whereby the user can hear how a word is pronounced. Specialized dictionaries in all fields can be found in cyberspace. From medical terminology to foreign languages, Web searchers can find vocabulary help for almost all their needs.

Unabridged Dictionaries A dictionary that is unabridged is the most complete. The most complete unabridged dictionary of the English language is the *Oxford English Dictionary (OED)*. It is expensive—with a list price of $3,000—so it is available only in libraries. The second edition comprises twenty volumes and lists approximately 500,000 words, many more than even the most complete collegiate dictionary. In addition to many more words, it also contains more meanings for each word and information about word history and usage. You may need to refer to an unabridged dictionary to find an unusual word or an unusual meaning, to check a word's origin, or to check the various prefixes or suffixes that can be used with a particular word. You can visit the OED Web site (http://www.oed.com), for a visual tour of the dictionary.

Tips for Using a Dictionary

Since you will have hundreds of occasions to use a dictionary throughout your college career, you should learn to use it efficiently. A dictionary is a wonderful resource, and it contains much more than just word meanings. The first step in using a dictionary effectively is to become familiar with the kinds of information it provides. In the following sample entry, each kind of information is marked.

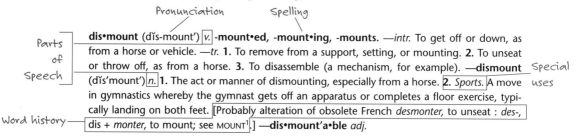

Pronunciation key and entries for "dismount," "dismiss," "familiar," "found 1," "found 2," and "oblique." Copyright © 2000 by Houghton Mifflin Company. Reproduced by permission from *The American Heritage Dictionary of the English Language,* Fourth Edition.

You can see that a dictionary entry includes information on a word's spelling, pronunciation, part of speech, history, and special uses.

Spelling Dictionary entries give the correct spelling of the words, including how to make words plural and how to add endings such as *-ed*, *-ing*, and so forth. They also give variant spellings (alternative acceptable spellings), as well as principal parts of verbs, and comparative and superlative forms of adjectives.

- **Plurals:** If the plural of a noun is irregular, the plural is given after the part of speech designation in the entry. If two plural spellings are acceptable, both will be given. For example, the plural of the word *criterion* will be shown as *pl. -teria or -terions.*

EXERCISE 1-1

Locate the plural of each of the following words.

EXAMPLE: potato <u>potatoes</u>

1. jockey <u>jockeys</u>

2. robbery <u>robberies</u>

3. alumnus <u>alumni</u>

4. radix <u>radices or radixes</u>

5. labellum <u>labella</u>

- **Derivatives:** Words formed by adding beginnings (prefixes) or endings (suffixes) to a base word are called *derivatives*. The words *preread* and *reading* are derivatives of the base word *read*. If you cannot find a derivative listed as an entry, look under the base word. Derivatives of a base word are often listed at the end of the entry. For example, if you cannot find the word *decreasingly* as its own entry, look under the entry for *decrease*.

EXERCISE 1-2

List at least two derivatives of each of the following base words. Answers will vary.
Some possibilities are listed.

EXAMPLE: man: <u>mankind, manmade, manhunt, chairman</u>

1. earn: <u>earnings, earner</u>

2. cohere: <u>cohesive, coherent, incoherent, cohesion</u>

3. act: <u>active, action, actor, actress, enact, react, reaction</u>

4. potent: <u>potential, impotent, potentate</u>

5. spirit: <u>spiritless, spirited, dispirited, spiritual</u>

- **Variant spellings:** Entries may include alternative acceptable spellings of words. The more accepted spelling is given first. The alternative spelling is designated by the word *also*, in italics. For example, an entry for the word *medieval* would say "*also* mediaeval."

EXERCISE 1-3

Locate a variant spelling for each of the following words.

EXAMPLE: judgment: <u>judgement</u>

1. glamorize: <u>glamourize</u>

2. esophagus: <u>oesophagus</u>

3. pilose: <u>pilous</u>

4. lachrymal: <u>lacrimal</u>

5. aerie <u>aery or eyrie or eyry</u>

- **Syllabication:** Each entry shows how the word is divided into syllables. This information is helpful in pronouncing words and when you must split and hyphenate a word that appears at the end of a printed line. (Hyphens are placed only between syllables.)
- **Principal parts of verbs:** For verbs, an entry may contain the verb's principal parts: past tense, past participle, present participle (if different from the past), and third person singular present tense. These parts use the endings, *-ed, -ing,* and *-es.* Some dictionaries list the principal parts of all verbs; others list the principal parts only if they are irregularly formed. The verb *write,* for example, is irregularly formed, and a dictionary entry would show the following parts: *wrote, written, writing, writes.*

EXERCISE 1-4

Locate the principal parts of each of the following verbs.

1. leave: <u>left, leaving, leaves</u>

2. lie <u>lay, lain, lying, lies</u>

3. throw: <u>threw, thrown, throwing, throws</u>

4. burst: <u>burst, bursting, bursts</u>

5. get: <u>got, gotten or got, getting, gets</u>

Pronunciation   The pronunciation for each entry word in a dictionary is shown in parentheses following the word. This pronunciation key shows you how to pronounce a word by spelling it the way it sounds. Different symbols are used to indicate certain sounds. The first step to using the pronunciation information is to learn to use the key that shows what the symbols mean and how they sound. The key appears on each page of the dictionary. Here is a sample key from the *American Heritage Dictionary of the English Language.*

ă pat	oi boy
ā pay	ou out
âr care	ŏŏ took
ä father	ōō boot
ě pet	ŭ cut
ē be	ûr urge
ĭ pit	th thin
ī pie	*th* this
îr pier	hw which
ŏ pot	zh vision
ō toe	ə about, item
ô paw	♦ regionalism

Stress marks: ˈ (primary); ˈ (secondary), as in **dictionary** (dĭkˈshə-nĕrˈē)

The key shows the sound the symbol stands for in a word you already know how to pronounce. For example, suppose you are trying to pronounce the word *helix* (hēˈlĭks). The key shows that the letter *e* in the first part of the word sounds the same as the *e* in the word *be.* The *i* in *helix* is pronounced the same way as the *i* in *pit.* To pronounce a word correctly, you must also accent (or put stress on) the appropriate part of the word. In a dictionary respelling, an accent mark (ˈ) usually follows the syllable, or part of the word, that is stressed most heavily.

Examples

audience	ô′dē-əns
football	fŏŏt′bôl′
homicide	hŏm′ĭ-sīd′
hurricane	hûr′ĭ-kān′

Some words have two accents—a primary stress and a secondary stress. The primary one is stressed more heavily and is printed in darker type than the secondary accent.

interstate	ĭn′tər-stāt′

The syllables with no accent marks are unstressed syllables. The vowel sounds in these unstressed syllables are often marked with a symbol that looks like an upside down letter *e*. It is called a schwa sound (ə). The schwa sound stands for sounds that can be spelled by any vowel or combination of vowels. The schwa stands for the blurred sound of "uh." Listen to it in each of the following words:

alone	ə-lon′
nickel	nik′əl
collect	kə-lect′

Try to pronounce each of the following dictionary respellings, using the pronunciation key:

dĭ-vûr′sə-fī′	bŏŏsh′əl
chăl′ənj	bär′bĭ-kyōō′

EXERCISE 1-5

Use the pronunciation key above to sound out each of the following words. Write the word, spelled correctly, in the space provided.

1. sfĭr sphere

2. wûr′kə-bəl workable

3. prĕj′ə-dĭs prejudice

4. nīt′mâr′ nightmare

5. dĭ-lĭsh′əs delicious

Part(s) of Speech   The part of speech, which follows the entry word's pronunciation, is given as an italicized abbreviation (*n.* for noun, *pron.* for pronoun, *v.* for verb, *adj.* for adjective, *adv.* for adverb, *prep.* for preposition, *conj.* for conjunction, and *inter.* for interjection). Verbs may be identified as either transitive (*tr.*) or intransitive (*intr.v.*). Transitive verbs are action verbs that direct their action at someone or something and are followed by a direct object (She **wrote** the poem, He **lifts** weights). Intransitive verbs do not need a person or thing to complete the meaning of the sentence in which they are used (He **lied**, She **cries**). Intransitive verbs do not take a direct object.

Many words can function as more than one part of speech. For example, *train* can be both a noun and a verb. When a word can be used as more than one part of speech, the meanings for each part are grouped together, as shown in the above entry for the word *dismount*. It can function either as a transitive or intransitive verb.

For each of the following words, indicate at least two parts of speech for which it can be used.

EXAMPLE: lapse   verb, noun

1. contract   noun, verb

2. right   adjective, noun, adverb, verb

3. pinch   verb, noun, adjective

4. quarter   noun, adjective, verb

5. each   adjective, pronoun, adverb

Definitions   Some dictionaries arrange word meanings in an entry chronologically, with the oldest meaning first. *Webster's Ninth Collegiate Dictionary,* for example, arranges meanings with the oldest known meaning first. *Merriam-Webster's Collegiate Dictionary* also lists words historically. (This dictionary is available online at http://www.m-w.com/dictionary.htm). Other dictionaries, such as the *American Heritage Dictionary of the English Language,* arrange meanings in order of most common usage. The sample entry on page 11 arranges meanings by how commonly they are used.

Etymology   Many dictionaries include information on each word's etymology— the origin and development of a word, including its history traced back as far as possible to its earliest use, often in another language. The sample dictionary entry below shows that the word *dismiss* was derived from Middle English.

Find the origin of each of the following words in a dictionary and write it in the space provided.

EXAMPLE: vanilla   Spanish

1. continue   Middle English/Old French/Latin

2. granite   Italian/Latin

3. jaunty   French

4. charisma   Greek

5. sauna   Finnish

Subject Labels
Many dictionaries include subject labels that show how a word is being used for a specific topic or field of study. Often called restrictive meanings as well, they define a word as it is used in a particular academic discipline. The subject area in which the word is used is printed in italic type followed by the meaning of the word in that particular discipline. The following entry for *dismiss* shows the meaning of the word in law and in sports. If you found this word in a legal document, you would focus on the first subject label, while physical education majors would find the second subject label more useful.

dis•miss (dĭs-mĭs′) *tr.v.* **-missed, -miss•ing, -miss•es. 1.** To end the employment or service of; discharge. **2.** To direct or allow to leave: *dismissed troops after the inspection; dismissed the student after reprimanding him.* **3.a.** To stop considering; rid one's mind of; dispel: *dismissed all thoughts of running for office.* **b.** To refuse to accept or recognize; reject: *dismissed the claim as highly improbable.* **4.** *Law.* To put (a claim or action) out of court without further hearing. **5.** *Sports.* To put out (a batter) in cricket. [Middle English *dismissen,* from Medieval Latin *dismittere, dismiss-,* variant of Latin *dīmittere* : *dī-, dis-,* apart: see DIS- + *mittere,* to send.] —**dis•miss′i•ble** *adj.* —**dis•mis′sion** (-mĭsh′ən) *n.*

- **Bundling**

  Old: A form of courtship in bed in which lovers are tied up or bundled to prevent undue familiarities

  New: Selling elements of a computer system as a package to eliminate competition

- **SPAM**

  Old: A canned meat made from spiced ham

  New: Junk e-mail

- **Cookie**

  Old: A small Dutch cake served as a dessert

  New: A text file placed on a computer hard drive by an Internet server to track a user's habits and tastes

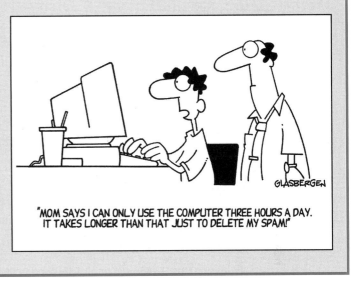

"MOM SAYS I CAN ONLY USE THE COMPUTER THREE HOURS A DAY. IT TAKES LONGER THAN THAT JUST TO DELETE MY SPAM!"

Source: "On Language" column by William Safire. "Bundling: Low-Tech Meanings find High-Tech Meanings." *The New York Times Magazine,* June 11, 2000, pp. 26, 28.

EXERCISE 1-8

For each of the following words, find the definition for the subject areas listed.

Word   Subject Areas

EXAMPLE:

band   Biology: a chromatically, structurally, or functionally differentiated strip or stripe in
                      or on an organism

            Anatomy: a cordlike tissue that connects or holds structures together

            Computer science: circular tracks on a storage device such as a disk

1. family   Linguistics: a group of languages descended from the same parent language

            Mathematics: a set of functions or surfaces that can be generated by varying the
            parameters of a general equation

            Chemistry: a group of elements with similar chemical properties or a vertical
            column in the periodic table of elements

2. mode   Music: any of certain fixed arrangements of the diatonic tones of an octave, as the major and minor scales of Western music

Philosophy: the particular appearance, form, or manner in which an underlying substance, or a permanent aspect or attribute of it, is manifested

Mathematics: the number or range of numbers in a set that occurs the most frequently

3. tonic   Physiology: of, relating to, or producing tone or tonicity in muscles or tissue

Medicine: characterized by continuous tension or contraction of muscles

Music: the first note of a diatonic scale; the keynote

4. nucleus   Botany: the central kernel of a nut or seed

Anatomy: a group of specialized nerve cells or a localized mass of gray matter in the brain or spinal cord

Astronomy: the central portion of the head of a comet

5. charge   Law: to instruct (a jury) about the law, its application, and the weighing of evidence, or to make a claim of wrongdoing against; accuse or blame

Physics: to cause formation of a net electric change on or in (a conductor, for example), or to energize (a storage battery) by passing current through it in the direction opposite to discharge

Accounting: to consider or record as a loss

Synonyms   Desk dictionary entries often list synonyms—words that have similar meanings—for entry words and explain the differences in meanings among the synonyms. The synonyms given in the entry below for the word *familiar* are followed by the shared meaning: "These adjectives describe relationships marked by intimacy." Then the different shades of meaning for each synonym are described: "Familiar implies . . . ," "Close implies . . . ," and so forth.

fa•mil•iar (fə-mĭl′yər) *adj. Abbr.* **fam. 1.** Often encountered or seen; common. **2.** Having fair knowledge; acquainted: *was familiar with those roads.* **3.** Of established friendship; intimate: *on familiar terms.* **4.** Natural and unstudied; informal: *lectured in a familiar style.* **5.** Taking undue liberties; presumptuous: *Students should not try to be familiar in their behavior toward an instructor.* **6.** Familial. **7.** Domesticated; tame. Used of animals. —**familiar** *n. Abbr.* **fam. 1.** A close friend or associate. **2.** An attendant spirit, often taking animal form. **3.** One who performs domestic service in the household of a high official. **4.** A person who frequents a place. [Middle English, from Old French *familier,* from Latin *familiāris,* domestic, from *familia,* family. See FAMILY.] —**fa•mil′iar•ly** *adv.*

SYNONYMS: familiar, close, intimate, confidential, chummy. These adjectives describe relationships marked by intimacy. *Familiar* implies an easy, often informal association based on frequent contact or shared interests: *a familiar song; a familiar guest. Close* implies strong emotional attachment: *close friendship; close to my brothers and sisters. Intimate* suggests bonds of affection or understanding resulting from the sharing of interests, problems, and experiences: *intimate friends; on an intimate footing. Confidential* suggests closeness founded on trust: *the prime minister's confidential secretary. Chummy* implies the comfortable, casual sociability shared by close friends: *The bartender was chummy with the regular customers.*

For each of the pairs or sets of synonyms listed below, explain the difference in meaning.

EXAMPLE: subject, topic: both denote the principal idea or point of a speech, a piece of writing, or an artistic work; *subject* is the more general term, whereas *topic* is a subject of discussion, argument, or conversation

1. form, figure, shape: All refer to the external outline of a thing, but *form* is its outline and structure as opposed to its substance; *figure* refers to form as established by bounding or enclosing lines; *shape* implies three-dimensional definition indicating both outline and bulk or mass.

2. bright, brilliant, radiant: All refer to what emits or reflects light, but *bright* is the most general; *brilliant* implies intense brightness and sparkling, glittering, or gleaming light; *radiant* radiates or seems to radiate light.

3. offend, insult: Both mean to cause resentment, humiliation, or hurt, but *offend* is to cause displeasure, hurt feelings, or repugnance in another; *insult* implies gross insensitivity, insolence, or contemptuous rudeness resulting in shame or embarrassment.

4. perform, accomplish, achieve: All mean to carry through to completion, but *perform* is to carry out an action, observing due form or exercising skill or care; *accomplish* connotes the successful completion of something requiring tenacity or talent; *achieve* is to accomplish something through effort or despite difficulty, implying a significant result

5. complex, complicated: Both mean having parts so interconnected as to make the whole perplexing, but *complex* implies a combination of many associated parts, whereas *complicated* stresses elaborate relationship of parts.

Homographs Homographs are words that have the same spelling but different meanings and different origins. An example would be the words *prune* (as in *prune* juice) and *prune* (as in *prune* the fruit trees). Homographs are identified by raised numbers called *superscripts* following the entry.

The word *found* is a homograph. It has three distinct meanings, as shown below.

found[1] (found) *tr.v.* **found•ed, found•ing, founds. 1.** To establish or set up, especially with provision for continuing existence: *The college was founded in 1872.* **2.** To establish the foundation or basis of; base: *found a theory on firm evidence.* [Middle English *founden,* from Old French *fonder,* from Latin *fundāre,* from *fundus,* bottom.]

SYNONYMS: found, create, establish, institute, organize. The central meaning shared by these verbs is "to bring something into existence and set it in operation": *founded a colony; created a trust fund; establishing an advertising agency; instituted an annual ball to benefit the homeless; organizing the metal-trading division of a bank.*

found[2] (found) *tr.v.* **found•ed, found•ing, founds. 1.** To melt (metal) and pour into a mold. **2.** To make (objects) by pouring molten material into a mold. [Middle English *founden,* from Old French *fondre,* from Latin *fundere.* See **gheu-** in Appendix.]
found[3] (found) *v.* Past tense and past participle of **find.**

Explain the meaning of each of the following homographs.

EXAMPLE: former   one that forms / occurring earlier in time

1. gyro a gyroscope / a sandwich

2. pink a color / to prick / a sailing vessel

3. quail a bird / to shrink back in fear

4. tender fragile / a formal offer / one who tends something

5. splat a slat of wood, as in a chair back / a smacking noise

Abbreviations   All dictionaries provide a key to abbreviations used in the entry itself. Most often this key appears on the inside front cover or on the first few pages of the dictionary. Dictionaries also contain information on how to abbreviate common words and phrases. You can look up an abbreviation and find the word or phrase it stands for, or you can look up a word and find its abbreviation. Abbreviations are labeled "abbr." For example, the entry for the abbreviation *lb.* indicates that it is an abbreviation for *libra*, an ancient Roman weight, and for *pound*, a modern measurement of weight.

For each of the following abbreviations, list the word or phrase it represents.

EXAMPLE: LDL   low-density lipoprotein

1. EPROM erasable-programmable read only memory

2. RDA recommended daily allowance

3. POE port of entry

4. MRI magnetic resonance imaging

5. NATO North Atlantic Treaty Organization

For each of the following words or phrases, locate its abbreviation.

EXAMPLE: Joint Chiefs of Staff   J.C.S. or JCS

1. educational television ETV

2. surface-to-air missile SAM

3. kilowatt kW

4. horsepower hp

5. Attorney General Att. Gen.

Idioms   An idiom is a phrase that has a meaning other than what the common meaning of the words in the phrase mean. For example, the phrase "turn over a new leaf" is not about the leaves on a tree. It means to *start fresh* or *begin over again* *in a new way.* You can locate idioms in a dictionary by looking under the key words in the phrase. To find the meaning of the idiom *as the crow flies,* look under the entry for *crow.* Idioms are usually identified by the label "—idiom," followed by the complete phrase and its meaning.

EXERCISE 1-13

Circle the answer that best explains the meaning of each of the following idioms.

1. to keep tabs on
   a. to encourage or promote
   b. to observe carefully
   c. to keep secret
   d. to compliment

2. to steal someone's thunder
   a. to ask someone for help
   b. to make someone look foolish
   c. to form an opinion about someone's behavior
   d. to use someone else's idea without his or her consent

3. to make no bones about
   a. to be forthright and candid about
   b. to withhold important information
   c. to pretend to understand a situation
   d. to live humbly or modestly

4. in the dark
   a. uninhabited
   b. alone or friendless
   c. uninformed
   d. fearful

5. to bite the bullet
   a. to defend one's actions
   b. to face a painful situation bravely
   c. to undergo a transformation
   d. to control one's temper

Other Useful Information Many dictionaries, especially desk dictionaries, contain numerous types of information. You may find entries for geographic places (*Mexico City*), historical figures (*Napoleon Bonaparte*), events (the *Civil War*), famous authors, artists, and composers (*Chaucer, van Gogh,* and *Mozart*). You also may find entries for literary and mythological illusions (*albatross, Hercules*).

EXERCISE 1-14

Use a dictionary to answer each of the following questions.

EXAMPLE: Where is Istanbul located?   Turkey

1. What color are the flowers on an ocotillo?   scarlet

2. For how many terms was Ulysses S. Grant president?   two

3. When did the Congo (Zaire) become independent?   1960

4. Who was Amphitrite's husband in Greek mythology?   Poseidon

5. What kind of dog is a Dandie Dinmont?   terrier

How to Locate Words Quickly

Most dictionaries use guide words to help you locate the page on which a particular word occurs. At the top of each dictionary page are two words in bold print, one on the left corner and one on the right. The guide word on the left is the first entry on that page; the one on the right is the last entry. All the words on that page come between the two guide words in alphabetical order. If the word you are looking for falls alphabetically between the two guide words on the page, scan that page to find the word. Suppose you are looking for the word *kinesics*. If your dictionary shows a page with the guide words *kindling* and *King of Prussia*, the word *kinesics* would be found there because, alphabetically, *kinesics* comes after *kindling* and before *King of Prussia*.

EXERCISE 1-15

Read each entry word and the pair of guide words that follows it. Decide whether the entry word would be found on the dictionary page with those guide words. Write *yes* or *no* in the space provided.

	Word	Guide Words	
EXAMPLE:	interstellar	interrogate—intervocalic	yes
1.	jaundice	jay—Jell-O	no
2.	chutney	chute—cilium	yes
3.	ooze	ontogenesis—open	yes
4.	quart	quant—quarry	no
5.	dragoman	dragonhead—drapery	no
6.	shallop	Shaker Heights—shambles	yes

How to Find the Right Meaning

Most words have more than one meaning. When you look up the meaning of a new word, you must choose the meaning that fits the way the word is used in the sentence context. Here are a few suggestions for choosing the correct meaning from among those listed in an entry:

1. If you are familiar with the parts of speech, try to use these to locate the correct meaning. For instance, if you are looking up the meaning of a word that names a person, place, or thing, you can save time by reading only those entries given after *n.* (noun).

2. In most types of academic reading, you can skip definitions that give slang and colloquial (abbreviated *colloq.*) meanings. Colloquial meanings refer to informal or spoken language.

3. If you are not sure of the part of speech, read each meaning until you find a definition that seems correct. Skip over the subject labels that are inappropriate.

4. Test your choice by substituting the meaning in the sentence with which you are working. Substitute the definition for the word and see whether it makes sense in the context.

Suppose you are looking up the word *oblique* to find its meaning in this sentence:

The suspect's **oblique** answers to the police officer's questions made her suspicious.

o•blique (ō-blēk′, ə-blēk′) *adj. Abbr.* **obl. 1.a.** Having a slating or sloping direction, course, or position; inclined. **b.** *Mathematics.* Designating geometric lines or planes that are neither parallel nor perpendicular. **2.** *Botany.* Having sides of unequal length or form: *an oblique leaf.* **3.** *Anatomy.* Situated in a slanting position; not transverse or longitudinal: *oblique muscles or ligaments.* **4.a.** Indirect or evasive: *oblique political maneuvers.* **b.** Devious, misleading, or dishonest: *gave oblique answers to the questions.* **5.** Not direct in descent; collateral. **6.** *Grammar.* Designating any noun case except the nominative or the vocative. —**oblique** *n.* **1.** An oblique thing, such as a line, direction, or muscle. **2.** *Nautical.* The act of changing course by less than 90°. —**oblique** (ō-blīk′, ə-blīk′) *adv.* At an angle of 45°. [Middle English, from Old French, from Latin *oblīquus.*] —o•blique′ly *adv.* —o•blique′ness *n.*

Oblique is used in the above sentence as an adjective. Looking at the entries listed after *adj.* (adjective), you can skip over the definition under the heading *Mathematics,* as it wouldn't apply here. Definition 4a (indirect or evasive) best fits the way *oblique* is used in the sentence.

EXERCISE 1-16

Each of the following sentences contains a boldfaced word that has several possible meanings. Circle the answer that identifies the meaning that is appropriate for the way the word is used in the sentence.

1. The engineer discovered an **obscure** flaw in the building's design.
   a. inconspicuous
   b. dark
   c. humble
   d. vague

2. Her father took a **dim** view of her decision to major in political science.
   a. indistinct
   b. negative or disapproving
   c. dull
   d. faint

3. The recent surge in the stock market has many investors feeling **flush**.
   a. level
   b. embarrassed
   c. feverish
   d. affluent

4. The musicians agreed to play at the bluegrass festival for **scale**.
   a. a minimum wage fixed by contract
   b. a progressive classification
   c. a system of ordered marks
   d. a series of tones

5. A **knot** of onlookers had formed even before the police arrived.
   a. a fastening
   b. a unifying bond
   c. a tight cluster
   d. a complex problem

6. The shortstop caught the baseball and threw the runner out in one **fluid** motion.
   a. a continuous substance
   b. smooth and flowing; graceful
   c. readily reshaped; pliable
   d. tending to change

7. My son likes every kind of cookie, but he is **partial** to Oreos.
   a. incomplete
   b. affecting only a part
   c. prejudiced
   d. having a particular fondness for something

Tips for Using a Thesaurus

A thesaurus is a dictionary of synonyms. It groups words with similar meanings together. A thesaurus is particularly useful when you want to

- Locate the precise term to fit a particular situation
- Find an appropriate descriptive word
- Replace an overused or unclear word
- Convey a different or more specific shade of meaning

Suppose you are looking for a more precise word for the expression *look into* in the following sentence:

> The marketing manager will **look into** the decline of recent sales in the Midwest.

The thesaurus lists the following synonyms for "look into":

look into [*v.*] *check, research*
audit, check out, delve into, dig, examine, explore, follow up, go into, inquire, inspect, investigate, look over, make inquiry, probe, prospect, scrutinize, sift, study;
SEE CONCEPT **103**

Read the above entry and underline words or phrases that you think would be more descriptive than *look into*. You might underline words and phrases such as *examine, scrutinize,* and *investigate*.

The most widely used thesaurus is *Roget's Thesaurus*. Inexpensive paperback editions are available in most bookstores. *Merriam-Webster's Collegiate Thesaurus* is available free online (http://www.m-w.com/thesaurus.htm).

When you first consult a thesaurus, you will need to familiarize yourself with its format and learn how to use it. The following is a step-by-step approach:

1. Many thesauri are organized alphabetically, much like a dictionary. Begin by locating the word you are trying to replace. Following the word, you will find numerous entries that list the synonyms of that word. Select words that seem like possible substitutes. (The hardback edition of *Roget's* is organized by subject with an index in the back.)

2. Test each of the words you selected in the sentence in which you will use it. The word should fit the context of the sentence.

3. Select the word that best expresses what you are trying to say.

4. Choose only words whose shades of meaning you know. Check unfamiliar words in a dictionary before using them. Remember, misusing a word is often a more serious error than choosing an overused, vague, or general one.

Using a thesaurus, replace the boldfaced word or phrase in each sentence with a more precise or descriptive word. Write the word in the space provided. Rephrase the sentence, if necessary.
Answers will vary.

EXAMPLE: The union appointed Corinne Miller to act as the **go-between** in its negotiations with management. _____ liaison _____

1. The two interviewers **went back and forth** asking questions of the candidate.
   _____ alternated _____

2. On the night of the inauguration, the ballroom looked **very nice**.
   _____ festive _____

3. More than anything, he **wanted** a new minivan. _____ desired _____

4. The town had gone through an economic decline, but now it appeared to be on the verge of an **increase**. _____ boom _____

5. The two brothers were opposites: Chester **liked to talk a lot**, whereas John was content to sit quietly and listen. _____ was talkative _____

6. Freshwater lakes that are in the process of accelerated eutrophication are often **cloudy-looking**. _____ milky _____

7. Daylilies range in color from **dark red** to yellow to almost white. _____ burgundy, ruby _____

8. Today's trend toward casual clothing in the workplace has made the demand for high-quality custom suits **fall**. _____ decrease, plummet _____

9. The children were **so sad** over the loss of their old dog Chumley. _____ sorrowful, doleful, desolate _____

10. The first speaker was interesting, but the second one was so **dull** I almost fell asleep.
    _____ colorless, pedestrian, uninspiring, stodgy _____

Tips for Using a Subject Dictionary

Specialized dictionaries that list most of the important words in a particular discipline are called *subject dictionaries*. They list technical and specialized meanings for words used in the particular field of study and suggest how and when to use them. For the fields of medicine and nursing, for example, there is *Taber's Cyclopedic Medical Dictionary*. Other subject dictionaries include *The New Grove Dictionary of Music and Musicians* and a *Dictionary of Economics*. Most subject dictionaries are available only in hardback; look for them in the reference section of your library. However, many are available online, either through a library that subscribes to them or as a free Web site. For a comprehensive directory of online subject dictionaries, visit the following Web site: http://www.yourdictionary.com/specialty.html. (Note that this is a commercial site, and it is unclear whether entries have been academically evaluated before they are included.)

Use a subject dictionary when you are unclear about the meaning of a term as used in your textbook and its glossary. You might also refer to a subject dictionary when you want to learn the distinction between several similar terms or when you want to learn more about the history and usage of a term.

List the courses you are taking this semester. For three of your courses, find the name of a subject dictionary and evaluate its usefulness.

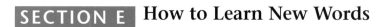

_____

_____

_____

_____

_____

SECTION E   How to Learn New Words

Remember the weekly spelling and vocabulary lists you used to get in school? The list was distributed on Monday; the test was on Friday. (Why are tests always on Friday?) After passing the test you forgot the words, right? Memorization is obviously the wrong way to learn new vocabulary. This section will show you two better ways.

The Index Card System

As you read textbook assignments and reference sources, and while listening to your instructors' class presentations, you are constantly exposed to new words. Unless you make a deliberate effort to remember and use these words, many of them will probably fade from your memory. One of the most practical and easy-to-use systems for expanding your vocabulary is the index card system. It works like this:

1. Whenever you hear or read a new word that you intend to learn, jot it down in the margin of your notes or mark it some way in the material you are reading.

2. Later, write the word on the front of an index card. Then look up its meaning and write it on the back of the card. Also, record a phonetic key for the word's pronunciation, its part of speech, other forms the word may take, and a sample sentence or example of how the word is used. If you are a visual learner, draw a diagram or picture to depict the word, as well. Your cards should look like the one in Figure 1-1, on page 19.

3. Once a day, take a few minutes to go through your pack of index cards. For each card, look at the word on the front and try to recall its meaning on the back. Then check the back of the card to see whether you were correct. If you were unable to recall the meaning or if you confused the word with another word, retest yourself. Shuffle the cards after each use.

4. After you have gone through your pack of cards several times, sort the cards into two piles—words you know and words you have not learned. Then, putting the known words aside, concentrate on the words still to be learned.

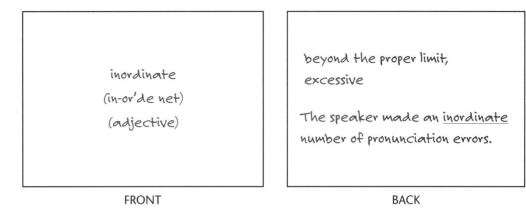

FRONT   BACK

FIGURE 1–1   Sample index card.

5. Once you have learned the entire pack of words, review them often to refresh your memory.

This index card system is effective for several reasons. First, it can be reviewed in the spare time that is often wasted waiting for a class to begin, riding a bus, and so on. Second, the system enables you to spend time learning what you do *not* know rather than wasting time studying what you already know. Finally, the system overcomes a major problem that exists in learning information that appears in list form. If the material to be learned is presented in a fixed order, you tend to learn it in that order and may be unable to recall individual items when they appear alone or out of order. By shuffling the cards, you scramble the order of the words and thus avoid this problem.

A Vocabulary Log

A vocabulary log is a list of words you want to learn. They may be words that you find in textbooks, articles and essays, or magazines in newspapers. You might also record words you heard in class lectures. Be sure to record only useful words—those you want to learn. You can use a variety of formats. You can create a vocabulary log for each course you are taking, reserving a section in each of your notebooks in which you record lecture notes. You can keep a separate notebook and designate it as your vocabulary log. You can create a computer file or files.

In addition to recording words and their meanings, be sure to record each word's pronunciation if it is not familiar. Some students also record a sentence using the word. Others include a text reference page number so they can locate where they first found the word. Experiment with different formats and different organizations until you find one that works for you. An excerpt from one student's vocabulary log for psychology is shown in Figure 1-2.

EXERCISE 1-19

Create an index card file or vocabulary log for one of your other courses. Update it weekly.

Word	Meaning	Page
intraspecific aggression	attack by one animal upon another member of its species	310
orbitofrontal cortex	region of the brain that aids in recognition of situations that produce emotional responses	312
modulation	an attempt to minimize or exaggerate the expression of emotion	317
simulation	an attempt to display an emotion that one does not really feel	319

FIGURE 1–2 Vocabulary log for a psychology course.

SECTION F Use It or Lose It! A System for Using the Words You Learn

The bad news: Forgetting happens! If you don't play a sport for several years, you forget some of the plays and moves and have to relearn them. If you don't perform a certain function on your computer for several months, you forget the commands to use. If you don't use a new word you just learned, you are likely to forget it.

The good news: You can prevent it.

Here are some suggestions for learning and retaining words. Depending on your learning style, some of the suggestions will work better than others.

- Write the word immediately. If you find the word in a textbook, you will have a better chance of remembering it if you write it rather than just highlight it. In fact, write it several times, once in the margin of the text, then again on an index card or in your vocabulary log. Write it again as you test yourself.

- Write a sentence using the word. Make the sentence personal, about you or your family or friends. The more meaningful the sentence is, the more likely you are to remember the word.

- Try to visualize a situation involving the word. For instance, for the word *restore* (to bring back to original condition), visualize an antique car restored to original condition.

- Draw a picture or diagram that involves the word. For example, for the word *squander* (to waste), draw a picture of yourself squandering money by throwing dollar bills out an open car window.

- Talk about the word. With a classmate, try to hold a conversation in which each of you use at least ten new words you have learned. Your conversation may become comical, but you will get practice using new words.

- Try to use the word in your own academic speech or writing as soon as you have learned it.
- Give yourself vocabulary tests or, working with a friend, make up tests for each other.

EXERCISE 1-20

For words in your index card file or vocabulary log, experiment with the above suggestions. List below two suggestions that seem to work well for you.

1. _____

2. _____ ▪

Once you have learned a new word, make sure you can spell it correctly. To learn the spelling of a word, use these four steps:

1. Look for familiar parts in a word. When you see the word *budgetary*, you can see the word *budget*, for example. Is it spelled in a similar way to another word you already know? *Perceive* is spelled in a similar way to *receive*, for example. The more meaningful you can make the word's spelling, the easier it will be to remember it.

2. Say the word aloud and copy it as you speak. Copy it several more times.

3. Try to write the word without looking at the original word.

4. Check to see if you spelled it correctly. If not, repeat the above steps until you can spell it correctly.

Keep a list or log of words you have misspelled on papers or exams. Work on learning each word on the list. Periodically, test yourself to see if you can still spell each one correctly.

SECTION G — You Are What You Eat: A Daily Menu of New Words

What happens when you eat an orange popsicle? Your tongue turns orange! You are what you eat. To stay or become a healthy person, you have to pay attention to what you eat. A daily diet of new words will help you become a well-spoken individual and an effective writer.

Here are five easy ways to introduce new words into your diet:

- Be alert for words that you know but do not use. There are hundreds of words that you recognize when you read or listen, but do not use yourself. Make note of useful words that would sharpen your own speech or writing. Add them to your index card file or vocabulary log.

- Keep an eye out for precise words that will replace two to three smaller, less descriptive words. For example, instead of *to take out*, consider words such as *remove* or *expunge*. Instead of *feeling sorry* about something, you could use the words *rue* or *regret*, *lament* or *bemoan* instead.

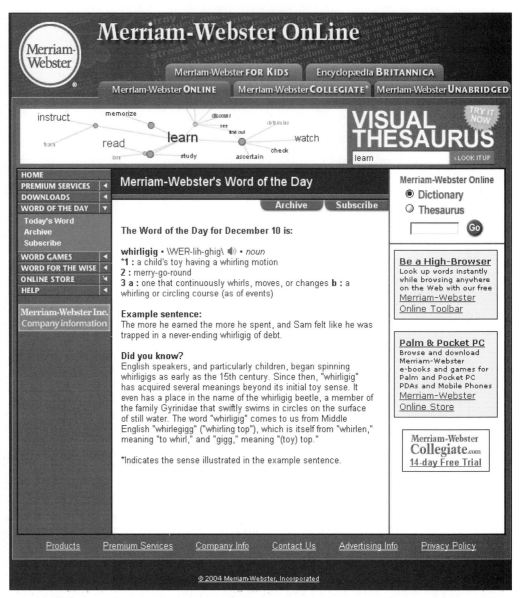

FIGURE 1–3 Merriam-Webster's word of the day.
From Merriam-Webster Online, www.Merriam-Webster.com. Copyright © 2004 Merriam-Webster, Inc. By permission.

- Look for additional meanings for words you already know. For example, you know that a *skirt* is an article of clothing, but you can also use it to mean to pass around or avoid, as in "The candidate *skirted* the controversial issue of gun control."

- Play word games. Various Websites offer word games that heighten your word awareness and introduce new words. The Merriam-Webster Website (http://www.m-w.com) offers a word game that changes daily.

- Learn a word each day. No matter how busy you are, find a new word to learn each day. If you aren't studying or attending classes, find a word on the TV news or in the newspaper. The Merriam-Webster Website also offers a "Word of the Day," as shown in Figure 1-3.

Applying and *Integrating* What You Have Learned

EXERCISE 1-21   APPLY YOUR SKILLS IN BIOLOGY

The following passage is taken from a biology textbook. The questions that follow illustrate situations in which you might apply the skills you have learned in this chapter. Answer each using a dictionary, thesaurus, or subject dictionary if needed.

To process food, an animal's body must provide an environment that favors the action of digestive enzymes. In addition, that environment must be contained in some type of compartment where the enzymes will not attack the organism's own macromolecules.

Even single-celled organisms have digestive compartments. Relatively simple animals such as hydras have a gastrovascular cavity, a digestive compartment with a single opening, the mouth. The gastrovascular cavity functions in both digestion and the distribution of nutrients throughout the body. A hydra's gastrovascular cavity enables it to ingest small crustaceans and other prey much larger than any of its cells could take in directly.

A hydra is a carnivore that stings its prey. It then uses its tentacles to stuff the food into its mouth, which expands to accommodate it. Once the prey is in the gastrovascular cavity, cells lining the cavity secrete digestive enzymes. Flagella on the cells keep the food mixed with the enzymes, and hydrolysis breaks down the soft tissues of the prey into tiny particles. Once the pieces are small enough, the cells lining the gastrovascular cavity engulf them into food vacuoles, where additional enzymes complete the digestion of the food into simple nutrient molecules. After the hydra has digested its meal, undigested materials remaining in the gastrovascular cavity are eliminated through the mouth.

—Adapted from Campbell, Mitchell, and Reece, *Biology: Concepts and Connections,* Third Edition, p. 432. Copyright © 2000. Reprinted by permission of Pearson Education, Inc.

1. Using an online subject dictionary, find the meaning of the following words:

    a. macromolecules: a giant molecule in a living organism: a protein, polysaccharide, or nucleic acid

    b. flagella: a long appendage that propels protists through the water and moves fluids across the surface of many tissue cells in animals

    c. hydrolysis: a chemical process in which macromolecules are broken down by the chemical addition of water molecules to the bonds linking their monomers; an essential part of digestion

2. Identify three words that would be useful to add to your index file or vocabulary log.
    Answers will vary.

3. Suppose you are writing a paraphrase—a word-for-word restatement of a passage using your own words. Use a dictionary or a thesaurus to find an appropriate synonym for each of the following words:

    a. ingest: eat or consume

    b. carnivore: an animal that eats other animals (or meat-eater)

    c. engulf: swallow up

4. Use a dictionary to find the correct pronunciation of each of the following words. In the space provided, write each word the way it sounds.

    a. gastrovascular: găs'trō-văs'kyə-lər

    b. crustacean: krŭ-stā'shən

    c. secrete: sĭ-krēt'

5. How is "gastrovascular cavity" defined in the passage?

    a digestive compartment with a single opening, the mouth

EXERCISE 1-22   SUBJECT DICTIONARY USAGE

For one of your courses, select three specialized words that appear in the glossary of your textbook and list them below.

Words: 1. _____ 2. _____ 3. _____

Using a subject dictionary, locate and read entries for the three words you selected above. Then answer the following questions:

1. In what ways did the subject dictionary differ from the glossary?

2. In what situations might you use a subject dictionary for this course?

EXERCISE 1-23   WORD GAME

Play the word game of the day on the Merriam-Webster Web site (http://www.m-w.com). Using the format of the game you played, create a new word game that would be useful for a classmate to play to improve his or her vocabulary.

LEARN MORE ABOUT BUILDING YOUR VOCABULARY by visiting the following Web sites:

1. Vocabulary: An Ongoing Process
   http://www.ucc.vt.edu/stdysk/vocabula.html

2. Commonly Misused Words
   http://www.cmu.edu/styleguide/trickywords.html#misused

3. A Word A Day
   http://www.wordsmith.org/awad/index.html

Endnotes

1. From "Survival of the Fittest" from *Directions* newsletter, 1997. Used by permission of DeVry Institute of Technology, a division of DeVry University.

2. From "English and Your Career," by Nancy Saffer, *Occupational Outlook Quarterly* 43, no. 2 (Summer 1999).

3. From "A World Where Language and 'Soft Skills' Are Key" by Sabra Chartrand, *New York Times*, April 6, 1997.

4. U.S. Department of Education, National Center for Education Statistics, National Adult Literacy Survey, 1992.

5. From *American Demographics* 17, no. 4:13 (April 1995).

PART TWO

Using Context to Figure Out Words

Making Educated Guesses About Word Meaning

What is the first thing you should do when you find a word you don't know?

- **Look it up in a dictionary? No.**

- **Analyze its parts? No.**

- **Skip it? No.**

- **Keep reading and try to figure out what the word means by the way it is used in the sentence? RIGHT!**

This part of the text will show you how to figure out what words mean by understanding the way they are used in the sentence or paragraph in which they appear. Often there are clues to the meaning of a word built into the sentence or paragraph that give you enough information to make at least an educated guess about meaning. Does this method work? Yes! And you have good odds that your guess is right, too, if you pay attention to these clues, known as *context clues*.

Let's see how and why this method works. Many sentences have more information in them than a reader or listener really needs. This is called *language redundancy*. Because no one can maintain 100 percent attention on a task for very long, writers and speakers naturally build extra clues into their speech and writing to help keep their audience on track. Try this experiment. Read the following paragraph and supply the missing words; read it through completely before you write anything.

Research conducted _____on_____ common foods such as orange juice, peach jelly, and strawberry sherbet shows that these foods were preferred when food coloring was added to ___improve___ their natural colors. For example, ___orange___ juice that was made to appear more orange _____was_____ preferred over ___regular___ orange juice. The ___researchers___ also found that the redder the _____juice_____ looked, the more appealing it was.

You did not have any trouble figuring out the missing words, right? From the words that were there, you knew what words were missing. How did you know? There were numerous clues. You could figure out some words from information that appeared earlier in the paragraph. Your knowledge of how English works helped, too. For example, you know that a noun (person, place, or thing) usually follows the word the *(the researchers)*. You know that the word that comes before juice was an adjective *(orange)* that describes it. Just as you could figure out missing words in the above paragraph, you will be able to figure out what some (but not all) unfamiliar words mean when you meet them while reading.

Types of Context Clues

The words that surround a word are called its *context*. Information about the meaning of a word that is contained in the surrounding words is called a *context clue*.

"THIS IS WHAT I GET FOR TRYING TO IMPROVE MY VOCABULARY"

Here are some quick tips for finding context clues:

- Don't stop reading as soon as you meet an unfamiliar word.
- Finish reading the sentence containing the unknown word. Many context clues follow the unknown word.
- If you can't find a context clue in the sentence containing the word, read the next couple of sentences. Context clues can appear anywhere in the paragraph.
- Once you do figure out the meaning of a word from its context, circle or highlight the word and jot down its meaning in the margin. Especially for textbooks that you are likely to review or reread, jotting down the meaning is especially important; you do not want to have to figure out a word's meaning all over again while reviewing.
- If you cannot find a context clue but can understand the meaning of the sentence without the meaning of the unknown word, keep reading. (You might want to mark the word with a question mark and check its meaning later.)

There are five types of context clues: (1) synonym, (2) definition, (3) example, (4) contrast, and (5) inference. You will learn how to use each in the following sections.

Synonym Context Clues

A group of friends is talking. Someone says, "Joining the Marines was a milestone in my life." Another friend says, "A what . . . ?" He replies, "you know, an important event." In speech, listeners can ask questions if they do not understand something. In writing, readers can't ask the writer questions, so writers must be careful to supply a clue, often a word or two, that suggests the meanings of words they think their readers might not know or may misunderstand. Often writers supply a *synonym*—a word or brief phrase that has a similar meaning. Here is an example. Can you tell what an asterism is by the underlined synonym?

An **asterism**, a <u>cluster of stars</u>, was visible last evening.

How to Spot Synonyms   Usually, the synonym immediately follows the word, as in the above example. Often it is set apart from the rest of the sentence using a linking word or phrase or by punctuation such as a comma, a dash, or parentheses. Common linking words are *or, also known as*, and *also called*.

Using a linking word: **Taste receptor cells**, also called <u>taste buds</u>, can identify four basic tastes: salty, sweet, bitter, and sour.

Using commas: The amateur figure skater **surpassed**, <u>or exceeded</u>, the judges' expectations.

Using dashes: The sculptor usually created a **maquette**—<u>a small model</u>—before beginning work on the actual piece.

Using parentheses: Thick layers of **loess** (<u>wind-blown silt</u>) cover regions of the Mississippi River valley.

You may also find a synonym for a word later in the paragraph, not even in the same sentence. This is a less common type of clue, but writers do use it occasionally.

Later in paragraph: Many companies have transferred labor-intensive operations to **maquiladoras** located along the U.S.-Mexican border. These <u>factories</u> that produce goods for export to the United States have created new jobs and contributed to economic growth.

EXERCISE 2-1

In each of the following sentences, underline the synonym for each boldfaced word.

EXAMPLE: The debate involved two **discrete**, <u>separate</u> issues.

1. Melanoma most commonly occurs in the **epidermis**, or <u>skin</u>.

2. We blamed our **lethargic**, <u>lazy</u> behavior on the oppressive heat.

3. The patient suffered **angina pectoris**—<u>severe chest pain</u>—before being admitted to the hospital.

4. Quill usually makes it her policy to **eschew**, or <u>avoid</u>, dessert.

5. The hummus recipe calls for **chickpeas**, also known as <u>garbanzos</u>.

6. After his accident and subsequent physical therapy, Luis decided to go into **kinesiology** (<u>the study of muscles</u>).

7. The coral snake is **indigenous**, or <u>native</u>, to tropical America and the southern United States.

8. Did you know that certain flowers, such as violas, are **esculent** (<u>edible</u>)?

9. The fishermen carried a **creel**—<u>a wicker basket</u>—to hold the fish they planned to catch.

10. The **remora**, also known as the <u>suckerfish</u>, can attach itself to sharks, whales, sea turtles, or the hulls of ships.

Revise each of the following sentences by adding a synonym context clue for the word in boldface. Use linking words, commas, dashes, and parentheses at least once in this exercise. Use a dictionary if necessary. Answers will vary. Some possibilities are given.

EXAMPLE: Jose listened to the **verbose** speaker discuss economic theories.

Jose listened to the **verbose,** talkative speaker discuss economic theories.

1. Ferdinand Magellan and his crew were the first people to **circumnavigate** the earth.

    Ferdinand Magellan and his crew were the first people to circumnavigate—travel completely

    around—the earth.

2. Jamil **prefaced** her speech with a poem by Derek Walcott.

    Jamil prefaced, or introduced, her speech with a poem by Derek Walcott.

3. Sheep typically **yean** in the spring.

    Sheep typically yean (bear young) in the spring.

4. The human **colon** is about 1.5 meters long.

    The human colon (the large intestine) is about 1.5 meters long.

5. The local garden club raised money for an extensive **instauration** of the park.

    The local garden club raised money for an extensive instauration, or renovation, of the park.

6. Many creative people find **architectonics** a fascinating subject.

    Many creative people find architectonics—the science of architecture—a fascinating subject.

7. **Periwinkle** is an excellent ground cover for shaded areas.

    Periwinkle (also known as myrtle) is an excellent ground cover for shaded areas.

8. The oldest **vertebrates** in the fossil record are fishlike fossils.

    The oldest vertebrates—animals with a backbone—in the fossil record are fishlike fossils.

9. We tried not to laugh while Henry was **castigated** for his poor manners.

    We tried not to laugh while Henry was castigated, or scolded, for his poor manners.

10. The **respiratory system** of premature babies is often underdeveloped.

    The respiratory system (breathing system) of premature babies is often underdeveloped.

Definition Context Clues

When writers are fairly certain their readers will not know a word they used, they include its definition. Definition context clues are especially common in textbooks where part of the author's purpose is to introduce and teach new terminology.

A **tariff** can be defined as a special tax imposed by the government on imported goods to raise the price, thus protecting American businesses and workers from foreign competition.

How to Spot Definition Clues   When giving a definition, writers usually use linking words such as *is (are)*, *is called*, *means*, *refers to*, and *can be defined as*. A comma rather than a linking word may be used if the definition is included as part of a sentence written for a purpose other than to simply define the term.

> *Using linking word:* **Advection** <u>is the horizontal movement and transfer of air or substances caused by wind or ocean currents</u>. [The sole purpose of this sentence is to define *advection*.]

> *Using comma:* Children under the age of two cannot grasp the concept of **conservation**, <u>the idea that physical objects remain constant despite changes in appearance</u>. [The purpose of this sentence is to explain that children less than two years old do not understand conservation; the definition of *conservation* is included as well.]

> *Using a dash:* **Relative humidity**—<u>a measure of the water content of the air</u>—is usually lower in warm afternoons and higher during cool evenings.

EXERCISE 2-3

Underline the definition clue that provides the meaning of the word in boldface.

EXAMPLE: **Hebephrenia**, <u>a mental disorder characterized by foolish mannerisms and senseless laughter</u>, may occur during adolescence.

1. **Telecommuting**, <u>working at home at a computer terminal</u>, has been linked to increased worker productivity.

2. **Genes**, <u>the hereditary units that determine an organism's traits and characteristics</u>, play an important role in biotechnology research.

3. **Dysphagia**—<u>difficulty in swallowing</u>—can be a symptom of strep throat.

4. Strangers often commented on the **sororal**, or <u>sisterly</u>, resemblance between the two girls.

5. **Acid precipitation**, usually defined as <u>rain or snow with a pH below 5.6</u>, is a result of fossil-fuel emissions.

6. Coran's parents were pleased to discover that he was truly **ambidextrous**, <u>able to use both hands equally well</u>.

7. **Dactylology**—more commonly known as <u>sign language</u>—relies on the use of a manual alphabet.

8. After James retired, he became a **docent**, or <u>tour guide</u>, at the state historical museum.

9. My grandmother's secret for her blue-ribbon fried chicken is **brining**—<u>soaking the chicken in salt water</u>—before frying.

10. The prosecutor accused the witness of giving **fallacious**, or <u>deliberately misleading</u>, testimony.

Revise each of the following sentences by adding a definition context clue for the word in bold-face. Use linking words, commas, and dashes at least once in this exercise. Use a dictionary if necessary. Answers will vary. Some possibilities are given.

EXAMPLE: The professor was in a **quandary** because she suspected some students had plagiarized, but she could not prove it.

               The professor was in a quandary, or predicament, because she suspected some students had plagiarized, but she could not prove it.

1. In humans, **oogenesis** occurs in the ovary.

   In humans, oogenesis—the formation of egg cells—occurs in the ovary.

2. The **temblor** registered 5.2 on the Richter scale.

   The temblor (earthquake) registered 5.2 on the Richter scale.

3. My music teacher taught me to look for terms such as **crescendo** and **rinforzando** in a piece of music.

   My music teacher taught me to look for terms such as crescendo (which means a gradual increase)

   and rinforzando (which means a sudden increase) in a piece of music.

4. The Manx cat can be described as **acaudate**, although it has an internal vestigial tail.

   The Manx cat can be described as acaudate (tailless), although it has an internal vestigial tail.

5. Gabriel lived in Paris long enough to become familiar with the city and its **environs.**

   Gabriel lived in Paris long enough to become familiar with the city and its environs,

   or surrounding areas.

6. The televangelist preached passionately against all forms of **iconolatry.**

   The televangelist preached passionately against all forms of iconolatry, the worship of icons or images.

7. Dr. Galyon plans to take a **sabbatical** at the end of this semester.

   Dr. Galyon plans to take a sabbatical, or leave of absence, at the end of this semester.

8. Most word processing programs allow you to automatically **paginate** reports and other documents.

   Most word processing programs allow you to automatically paginate, or number the pages

   of, reports and other documents.

9. Parker was invited to sing the national anthem **a cappella** before the Braves game.

   Parker was invited to sing the national anthem a cappella—without instrumental accompaniment—

   before the Braves game.

10. The candidate quickly became known for his **malapropisms** on the campaign trail.

    The candidate quickly became known for his malapropisms (misuse of words) on the campaign trail.

Example Context Clues

One of the easiest ways to explain something is to give an example or two. You can easily explain the term *road rage* by giving examples of angry driving behavior—cutting off other drivers, following at unsafe distances, honking the horn incessantly, and so forth. Examples often work better than definitions alone. Experienced writers know that many readers are pragmatic learners and need real, practical situations to help them understand an idea or concept. Often, then, if you are unfamiliar with a term, you can figure out what it means from the examples given.

> Some forms of **nonverbal communication,** <u>such as facial expressions, gestures, and posture,</u> are universally understood.

In this sentence, the examples of nonverbal communication suggest that it means body language or communication without words.

How to Spot Example Clues   Writers may use linking words such as *for example* or *for instance*. At other times, the example is built into the paragraph without linking words.

> *Using linking words:* **Opiates,** such as opium, morphine, and methadone, often seriously affect the emotional state of the user.

> *Without linking words:* The speaker made a **gaffe** when he referred to the women in the audience as "little ladies."

EXERCISE 2-5

In the space provided, write the letter of the choice that best states the meaning of the boldfaced word as it is used in the sentence.

1. Rachel explained her interest in **genealogy** in personal terms; for instance, she described the thrill of discovering that each of her great-grandparents arrived at Ellis Island in 1903.

   a. nature

   (b.) family history

   c. genes

   d. timetables

2. The comedian proved himself **impervious** to the response of the audience when he continued to tell jokes despite loud groans and cries of "Get off the stage!"

   a. sensitive

   (b.) unaffected

   c. disrespectful

   d. amused

3. Children between the ages of three and six sometimes suffer from a form of **parasomnia**, as evidenced by sleepwalking, night terrors, and bed-wetting.

   a. excitement

   b. anger

   (c.) sleep disorders

   d. daydreaming

4. Among the **denizens** of the tiny town were two lawyers, a physician, a veterinarian, and a schoolteacher.

   (a.) residents

   b. critics

   c. men

   d. women

5. For the damage they caused at the school, the teenagers have been ordered by the court to make **reparation**—specifically, they must paint over the graffiti and pay for new windows.

    a. remorse   c. obstruction

    b. liability   (d.) compensation

6. The purchase contract for the house included several **provisos;** for example, the interior of the house was to be painted and the roof replaced by the current owners.

    a. warnings   c. agreements

    (b.) conditions   d. questions

7. The health drink was advertised as a **panacea;** it promised to improve memory, boost energy levels, and relieve sleeplessness.

    a. dessert   (c.) cure-all

    b. prescription   d. supplement

8. Many wills include at least one **codicil,** such as an instruction about the disbursement of assets to stepchildren.

    (a.) addition   c. fee

    b. error   d. request

9. The fire marshal cited the building's owner for several **infractions;** for example, the fire escape was blocked and none of the smoke alarms worked.

    a. improvements   (c.) violations

    b. signs   d. supplies

10. To qualify for the gifted program, students must undergo a **battery** of tests designed to measure intelligence, creativity, and aptitude.

    (a.) series   c. connection

    b. requirement   d. question

EXERCISE 2-6

Read each sentence and write a definition or synonym for each boldfaced word or phrase. Use the example clue to help you determine the meaning. Answers will vary.

EXAMPLE: **Histrionics,** such as wild laughter or excessive body movements, are usually inappropriate in business settings. <u>exaggerated emotional behavior calculated for effect</u>

1. **Ethnic groups,** such as Chinese, Poles, and Italians, living in the United States have contributed much to its cultural diversity. <u>groups of people sharing a common heritage</u>

2. The school system recently received two **endowments,** one of $5,000 and one of $10,000, directed toward improvements in the art and music programs. <u>gifts of money</u>

3. Jacob's appetite for books is **voracious;** for instance, no sooner had he finished the latest Harry Potter book then he began reading *The Chronicles of Narnia* . <u>greedy or insatiable</u>

4. The opposition was quick to **propagate** rumors about the candidate; for example, his routine visit to the doctor was soon broadcast as "serious health concerns" over the Internet. <u>spread or publicize</u>

5. Susan's father suffered a series of **debilitating** strokes, leaving him partially paralyzed and unable to care for himself. <u>weakening or impairing</u>

6. The investigators accused the councilman of **obfuscating** the truth by destroying important records and threatening key witnesses. <u>obscuring</u>

7. Her workaholism and his infidelity were **precursors** to their divorce. <u>factors leading up to</u>

8. Even the positive aspects of a **sedentary** lifestyle, such as reading books and doing needle-work, should be balanced with an appropriate level of physical activity. <u>characterized by sitting</u>

9. The consultant proposed several **upgrades** to the current system, such as streamlined accounting procedures and automated inventory control. <u>improvements</u>

10. The company has several **auxiliary** locations, including stores in Georgia, Tennessee, and North Carolina. <u>supplementary or subsidiary</u>

EXERCISE 2-7

For each of the following words or phrases, write a sentence that provides an example context clue. Use a dictionary if necessary. Answers will vary.

EXAMPLE: martial arts <u>Martial arts, such as karate and judo, are growing in popularity.</u>

1. sport utility vehicles <u>Sport utility vehicles, including Ford Explorer and Jeep Cherokee, are not fuel efficient.</u>

2. dignitaries <u>Dignitaries, such as senators and governors, attended the ceremony.</u>

3. periodicals <u>Time and Newsweek, for example, are periodicals that feature national and international news.</u>

4. pop music stars <u>Pop music stars, such as Britney Spears and Jennifer Lopez, are growing in popularity, especially among families with small children.</u>

5. flowering trees <u>Flowering trees, including apple and pear, are welcome signs of spring.</u>

6. comedians <u>Comedians, such as Jay Leno and Jerry Seinfeld, remain popular.</u>

7. fast foods <u>Fast foods, burgers, fries, and pizza, for instance, are often high in calories.</u>

8. over-the-counter medications <u>Over-the-counter medications, including aspirin and ibuprofen, can give fast relief to minor health problems.</u>

9. spring break travel destinations <u>Popular spring break travel destinations usually include Florida and Cancun.</u>

10. aggressive behavior <u>Aggressive behavior, including fighting and kicking, is not tolerated on the playing field.</u>

Contrast Context Clues

It is sometimes possible to determine the meaning of a word from a word or phrase in the context that has an opposite meaning. In the following sentence, notice how the meaning of *depressants* provides a clue to the meaning of *stimulants*.

Unlike **stimulants**, <u>depressants slow functioning in the central nervous system.</u>

The word *unlike* tells us that depressants and stimulants are different. If depressants slow the functioning of the central nervous system, then stimulants speed up its functioning.

Basically, contrast clues require two steps. First you have to find a word that has the opposite meaning of the unknown word. Then you have to think of a word that has the opposite meaning of the context clue. Here are a few more examples.

Despite his reputation for **parsimony**, the old man left a <u>very generous</u> tip for the waitress.

In contrast to people with **myopia**, people with <u>hyperopia cannot focus at short distances.</u>

How to Spot Contrast Clues   In writing about two things or ideas that are different, writers often use linking words such as *but, although, on the other hand, yet, nevertheless, however, in contrast, while, unlike, even though, despite,* and so forth. These words signal that a contrasting, different idea is to follow.

EXERCISE 2-8

In the space provided, write the letter of the choice that best states the meaning of the boldfaced word as it is used in the sentence.

1. Despite her **penchant** for sweets, Maria was not tempted by any of the items on the dessert tray.

    (a.) fondness

    b. distaste

    c. diet

    d. intention

2. In contrast to this year's drought in the southern United States, the upper northwest had its most **pluvious** summer on record.

    a. dry

    b. remarkable

    (c.) rainy

    d. unpredictable

3. Although the composer intended it to be a happy, lighthearted piece of music, it sounded more like a **dirge** when it was performed by the choir.

    a. joyful tune

    (b.) funeral hymn

    c. performance

    d. recital

4. The starlet cultivated her image as a helpless and scatterbrained young woman, but in reality she was a **sagacious** businesswoman.

    a. independent

    (b.) shrewd

    c. unintelligent

    d. helpful

5. Every effort was made to ensure that the test was fair; nevertheless, several students complained that the questions were **skewed.**

    (a.) biased

    b. equal

    c. numerous

    d. too easy

6. In contrast to the former senator's long-winded, rambling speeches, his successor's comments were downright **pithy.**

    a. lengthy

    b. conservative

    c. unflattering

    (d.) brief

7. Unlike **perennial** plants, annuals complete their life cycle in a single season.

    a. tender

    b. winter-hardy

    c. blooming only once

    (d.) lasting more than one season, or recurring

8. While several aspects of the new charter school were open to discussion, the location of the new school was **immutable.**

    (a.) not subject to change

    b. unpleasant

    c. not decided

    d. debatable

9. This particular drug is often prescribed for its **soporific** effect; however, some patients have experienced sleeplessness upon taking it.

    a. stimulating

    (b.) sleep-inducing

    c. medical

    d. harmful

10. In dramatic contrast to the tropical temperatures of the Dominican Republic, Ramón found the climate in Iowa **hyperborean.**

    a. mild

    b. warm

    (c.) very cold

    d. similar

EXERCISE 2-9

Read each sentence and write a definition or synonym for each boldfaced word or phrase. Use the contrast clue to help you determine the meaning. Answers will vary.

EXAMPLE: Despite their seemingly **altruistic** actions, large corporations are self-interested institutions that exist to make profits. _unselfishness or selflessness_

1. City-dwellers often imagine that rural areas are peaceful at night, but the **cacophony** of insects and other night creatures can be deafening. _jarring, discordant sound; noise_

2. In contrast to the **levity** of the stockholders' meeting, the mood in the boardroom was sober. _lightness of manner or speech_

3. Although violence is **abhorrent** to most of us, certain forms of "street justice" have become somewhat acceptable in our society. _disgusting, repellent_

4. In contrast to **bradycardia**, tachycardia is a rapid heart rate of more than 100 beats per minute in an adult. _slow heart rate_

5. Although the store seemed to have a **plethora** of cowboy boots, there were none in his size.
abundance, plenty

6. Walter gave up alcohol every Sunday, yet by 10:00 on Friday night he was again in a state of **inebriety.** drunkenness

7. Although women are **enjoined** from serving as clergy in many mainstream churches, the Episcopal church is one that allows the ordination of female priests.
prohibited, forbidden

8. The tycoon was found guilty of tax evasion, but his wife was declared **inculpable.**
free of guilt, blameless

9. The lunchtime series has featured several entertaining speakers, although today's lecturer was much more **didactic.** instructive

10. When our criminal justice class interviewed inmates at the city's holding center, some were **hostile;** others were friendly and talkative. angry and uncooperative

Inference Context Clues

Many times, you can infer the meaning of an unknown word from the general meaning of the paragraph or passage in which it appears. Unlike the other context clues previously discussed, this type of clue does not depend on a particular word or phrase. Instead, from the overall sense of the passage and your own background knowledge or experience with the topic, you can figure out what a particular word means.

> After the playoff game, a **fracas** broke out among the fans of the losing team.

In the above sentence, you can reason that a *fracas* is a disorderly fight, quarrel, or brawl. From your background knowledge you know that brawls can break out among fans, and you know that playoff games may be particularly emotional or intense. The passage indicates that the fracas broke out among the fans of the losing team and, again, you know that fans of losing teams are likely to be disgruntled or unhappy.

Here is another example:

> After finding an **egregious error** on a recent statement, the auditor checked the company's accounts payable for the previous three years.

In this sentence, you can assume that an *egregious error* is a serious one if it caused the auditor to review three years' worth of accounts. *Serious* is close in meaning to the dictionary meaning of *egregious*, which is "conspicuously bad or offensive."

EXERCISE 2-10

In the space provided, write the letter of the choice that best states the meaning of the boldfaced word as it is used in the sentence.

1. The arrival of hurricane season was **heralded** by several small tropical storms in the Gulf of Mexico.

   a. prevented   c. announced

   b. studied   d. ended

2. Halfway through the horror movie, the fear in the audience was **palpable.**

   (a.) obvious
   b. terrifying

   c. humorous
   d. invisible

3. Many young people are leaving the state after graduation because of the **dearth** of good jobs in the area.

   a. offers
   b. abundance

   (c.) scarcity
   d. appearance

4. After her appearance in the highly successful low-budget film, the actress was **inundated** with offers.

   a. avoided
   (b.) swamped

   c. confused
   d. denied

5. Hugh finally decided that the **frenetic** pace of Wall Street wasn't for him and moved back to his family's farm in Vermont.

   a. slow
   b. financial

   c. calm
   (d.) frantic

6. Several factors **impeded** the progress of the new housing development, including zoning restrictions and opposition from landowners.

   a. encouraged
   b. allowed

   c. promoted
   (d.) obstructed or slowed

7. Her leopard-skin outfit at the humane society fundraiser was the **antithesis** of good taste.

   a. definition
   (b.) opposite

   c. design
   d. appearance

8. Before the third graders got off the bus at the museum, their teacher urged them to conduct themselves with **decorum.**

   (a.) polite behavior
   b. curiosity

   c. silence
   d. urgency

9. The press reported that the leaders of the two countries had reached a critical **juncture** in their negotiations.

   a. breakdown
   b. topic

   (c.) point
   d. debate

10. The prosecution presented a **cogent** argument, but the jury was not persuaded.

   (a.) convincing
   b. unclear

   c. deliberate
   d. weak

An eponym is a word that was formed from a person's name.

- Did you know that the words *teddy bear* came from the name of a U.S. president? President Theodore Roosevelt, nicknamed Teddy, was once shown in a cartoon sparing the life of a bear cub. From that cartoon, the words *teddy bear* evolved.

- A *Prince Charming* is a man who fulfills a woman's romantic dreams. Did you know that that term originally came from the hero of the fairy tale, "Cinderella"? Cinderella was rescued by Prince Charming.

- A *munchkin* is a very small, elflike person. Did you know that the word comes from the Munchkins, characters in *The Wonderful Wizard of Oz?*

Use a dictionary to discover from whom each of the following words originated.

1. sandwich   The Earl of Sandwich

2. cesarean section   Julius Caesar

3. leotard   Jules Leotard, a French aerialist

4. diesel engine   Rudolph Diesel, a German automotive designer

5. Doberman   Ludwig Doberman, a nineteenth-century dog breeder

Generall Mountague, since
Earle of Sandwich

The Earle of Sandwich and His Legacy.

EXERCISE 2-11

Read each sentence and write a definition or synonym for each boldfaced word or phrase. Use the general sense of the passage context clues to help you determine the meaning.

EXAMPLE: She was the **archetypal** grandmother: she brought wonderful presents, she told exciting stories, and her house always smelled of cookies.
ideal example; model

1. After an **auspicious** first novel, the writer turned out several books that were panned by the critics. _promising_

2. Because we had invited them to join us, we felt that the **onus** was on us to be sure that they had a good time. _burden, responsibility_

3. Many Americans considered President Clinton's behavior **flagrant**, although he ultimately survived the scandal. _shockingly bad; shameless_

4. The **pungent** smell of something burning greeted us as we walked in the door. _sharp-smelling; acrid_

5. To the police detective, the most **salient** aspect of the case was the suspect's lack of an alibi. _noticeable; obvious_

6. After playing in the yard all morning, the puppy was **inert** for the rest of the day. _inactive; motionless_

7. The topic of this month's journal is **vernacular** architecture unique to southern Mississippi. _characteristic of a particular region_

8. I thought the television program was **innocuous** until I saw some children acting out an especially violent episode. _harmless_

9. In an effort to **rectify** the situation, the manufacturer offered full refunds to dissatisfied customers. _correct; set right_

10. The toddler's parents tried to **dissuade** him from climbing on furniture, but to no avail. _discourage_

SECTION C What to Do When Context Doesn't Work

Try to use context to figure out the meaning of the underlined word in the following sentence.

The Italian director Federico Fellini was best known for his <u>surrealistic</u> films.

Give up? You should. There is no context clue to help you figure out what *surrealistic* **means.**

Using context is a great technique, but it does not always work. Not all sentences or paragraphs contain context clues. When you cannot find a context clue, then you have to use other methods to figure out a word's meaning. Here are some suggestions:

- Pronounce the word. Hearing it aloud may help you recall hearing or using the word before. Or, you may hear a word or part of a word within the unknown word that will ring a bell in your memory. For example, by pronouncing the word *predecessor*, you may recall your history professor using it in reference to presidential succession. Or, by pronouncing the word *deregulatory*, you may recognize the word *regulate*.

- If pronouncing the word does not help, then analyze the word's parts. This method is discussed in Part 3 of this text.

- If analyzing word parts does not work, then look up the word in your dictionary.

After Context, Then What?

Here today, gone tomorrow! This is what will happen to words that you figured out from context, unless you take steps to remember them.

Let's say you have figured out seven or eight meanings from context while reading a sociology chapter. Let's assume you jotted down each meaning in the margin of your sociology text, too. Now what should you do? If you think the words are useful additions to your general vocabulary or if the words are important words in sociology, then you should take the following steps.

Checking Exact Meanings

The first step is to check the exact meaning for any words you are unsure of. For example, in the following sentence, you may infer that *precipitately* means *quickly:*

Investors reacted **precipitately** to the news that the company's stock had fallen.

But if you check a dictionary, you would discover that a more precise meaning is *hastily* or *rashly.* Once you find a more accurate meaning, jot it down in the margin of your textbook.

EXERCISE 2-12

Use context to figure out the meaning of each of the words in boldface. In the space provided, write a brief definition or synonym. Then confirm or revise your definitions by checking each word's meaning in your dictionary.

EXAMPLE: Mia arrived on time for her class despite **adverse** travel conditions.

Bad ( ) confirmed   (X) need to revise (check one)

Revision: unfavorable

1. When a lecturer interjects **extraneous** information into the lecture, note taking becomes difficult.

   inessential or irrelevant_____ ( ) confirmed   ( ) need to revise (check one)

   Revision: _____

2. The computer we purchased in 2000 is well on its way to **obsolescence.**

   passing out of usefulness_____ ( ) confirmed   ( ) need to revise

   Revision: _____

3. Both parties were surprised to discover that the contract was **indefeasible.**

   cannot be annulled or voided_____ ( ) confirmed   ( ) need to revise

   Revision: _____

4. Because he had just become a father, Oscar was able to obtain a **deferment** of his military service.

   postponement   ( ) confirmed ( ) need to revise

   Revision: _____

5. The storm was severe, but the damage to our house was **negligible**.

   insignificant   ( ) confirmed ( ) need to revise

   Revision: _____

6. With friends in both places, Faye **vacillated** between the job offer in Raleigh and the one in Des Moines.

   wavered   ( ) confirmed ( ) need to revise

   Revision: _____

7. Dog-lovers have found that Newfoundlands make **stalwart** companions.

   strong or stout   ( ) confirmed ( ) need to revise

   Revision: _____

8. A **cabal** of religious extremists was responsible for the assassination attempt on the prime minister.

   a conspiratorial group of plotters; conspirators   ( ) confirmed ( ) need to revise

   Revision: _____

9. Her nephew gave her a **perfunctory** kiss on the cheek.

   indifferent   ( ) confirmed ( ) need to revise

   Revision: _____

10. The architect was known for his **minimalist** approach to design.

    use of the fewest and barest essentials or elements   ( ) confirmed ( ) need to revise

    Revision: _____

Adding Words to Your Index Card File or Vocabulary Log

Definitions recorded only in the margin of your textbooks are not convenient for review or study. For each word that you want to learn, add it and its meaning to your index card file or vocabulary log (see p. 19 or p. 20). You might also want to include a brief note indicating the title and page of the book in which you originally encountered the word.

EXERCISE 2-13

Update your index file or vocabulary log using words you have learned so far in this part of the book.

Applying and *Integrating* **What You Have Learned**

EXERCISE 2-14   APPLYING YOUR SKILLS IN AMERICAN HISTORY

Read the following passage and use context clues to figure out the meaning of each boldfaced word or phrase. Write a synonym or definition for each in the space provided. Consult a dictionary if necessary.

Martin Van Buren's brilliance as a political **manipulator**—the Red Fox, the Little Magician—has tended to **obscure** his statesmanlike qualities and his engaging personality. He made a powerful argument, for example, that political parties were a force for unity, not for **partisan** bickering. In addition, high office sobered him, and improved his judgment. He fought the Bank of the United States as a monopoly, but he also opposed irresponsible state banks. New York's Safety Fund System, requiring all banks to contribute to a fund, supervised by the state, to be used to **redeem** the notes of any member bank that failed, was established largely through his efforts. Van Buren believed in public construction of internal improvements, but he favored state rather than national programs, and he urged a **rational** approach: Each project must stand on its own as a useful and profitable public utility.

He continued to **equivocate** spectacularly on the tariff—in his *Autobiography* he described two of his supporters walking home after listening to him talk on the tariff, each convinced that it had been a brilliant speech, but neither having obtained the slightest idea as to where Van Buren stood on the subject—but he was never in the pocket of any special interest group or tariff **lobbyist**. He **accounted** himself a good Jeffersonian, tending to prefer state action to federal, but he was by no means **doctrinaire**. Basically he approached most questions rationally and **pragmatically**.

—Adapted from Garraty and Carnes, *The American Nation*, Tenth Edition, p. 267.

1. manipulator: <u>skilled at influencing other people to his own advantage</u>

2. obscure: <u>dim, darkened</u>

3. partisan: <u>biased in support of a political party</u>

4. redeem: <u>to pay off</u>

5. rational: <u>based on reason; logical</u>

6. equivocate: <u>to speak vaguely</u>

7. lobbyist: <u>one who attempts to influence public officials for or against a specific cause</u>

8. accounted: <u>considered</u>

9. doctrinaire: <u>inflexibly attached to a practice or theory without regard to its practicality; dictatorial</u>

10. pragmatically: <u>practically</u>

EXERCISE 2-15   APPLYING YOUR SKILLS IN BIOLOGY

Read the following passage and use context clues to figure out the meaning of each boldfaced word or phrase. Write a synonym or definition for each in the space provided.

The **canopies,** or treetops, of forests are one of nature's great **showplaces** of different kinds of living organisms. Biologists estimate that fully half of the 5 million to 50 million **species** on Earth spend all or much of their time here, yet canopies were virtually unexplored until about 15 years ago. The canopies of tropical rain forests, areas near the equator where yearly rainfall often exceeds 200 centimeters (80 inches), **harbor** the greatest number of species. Equally wet forests in the coastal regions of western Canada and the northwestern United States also are home to remarkable numbers. The **dominant** trees in many northern rain forests are centuries-old firs, hemlocks, and spruces. Extending into northern California are **remnants** of truly ancient rain forests dominated by redwoods and giant sequoia trees that are thousands of years old.

Research on forest canopies **blossomed** in the 1970s when scientists began using mountain climbers' roping techniques to reach the treetops. Roping techniques allow researchers to move from one area of forest to another, but they are not the only way to get into a canopy. For projects that can be done in a limited area, some researchers prefer large construction cranes with horizontal **booms** that rotate over the canopy. More permanent are platforms, walkways, and towers built into the treetops.

A summer evening is a good time to experience a canopy's rich **array** of life. In a rain forest in the northwestern U.S., brown and greenish fungi, lichens, and earthy mats of moss cling to the high branches. Your eye might catch the split-second shadow of a flying squirrel across a bright moon. Rarely seen because they are active only at night, these foot-long rodents speed-glide between the big trees. Insects are especially **abundant** in the canopy twilight, and bats flit about, often eating close to their own body weight in insects in a single night. Owls, another group of **nocturnal** hunters, are silent on the wing, but each species has its own **distinctive** hoot.

—Adapted from Campbell, Mitchell, and Reece, *Biology: Concepts and Connections*, Third Edition, p. 1. Copyright © 2000. Reprinted by permission of Pearson Education, Inc.

1. canopies: treetops

2. showplaces: beautiful or ornate places

3. species: biological categories

4. harbor: to provide a place, home, or habitat for

5. dominant: most prominent

6. remnants: remainders; surviving traces

7. blossomed: developed; flourished

8. booms: long, movable arms or poles

9. array: impressively large number; display

10. abundant: plentiful

11. nocturnal: most active at night

12. distinctive: serving to identify; distinguishing

EXERCISE 2-16   APPLYING YOUR SKILLS IN EDUCATION

Read the following passage and use context clues to figure out the meaning of each boldfaced word or phrase. Write a synonym or definition for each in the space provided.

Many psychologists maintain that contemporary life takes its toll on the human **psyche** in economically developed industrial nations, particularly among children. These observers suggest that the human mind may be better adapted to life in less "advanced" survival-centered societies. Various people once labeled "primitive" by Europeans lived in a state of harmony with nature, spending perhaps ten to fifteen hours a week finding food. While they lacked the luxuries of the contemporary Western world, they never **craved** such luxuries. After securing food, shelter and clothing, these **indigenous** peoples had time for rituals, reflection, community events and leisure. Although we must avoid the temptation to **romanticize** these people (they experienced serious illnesses and dangerous conflict and generally died young), they seemed able to escape boredom and malaise.

With its scientific gadgetry and technological wonders, **modernist** civilization promotes a regulated, intransigent pattern of existence that **represses** creative impulses. Neither school nor work in our society offers many **avenues** for creative **endeavor.** Perhaps the most important difference between traditional and modernist cultures appears in the daily lives of children. In traditional societies children spent the day with their parents and other community members participating in the activities of the group or clan. Constantly engaged, these young people learned throughout each day. By contrast, **contemporary** children find themselves removed from everyday **commerce,** sitting by themselves or in disconnected and bored bunches that countenance psychological difficulties and **pathological** behavior.

—Kincheloe, Slattery, and Steinberg, *Contextualizing Teaching*, pp. 68–69.

1. psyche: the spirit or soul

2. craved: longed for, desired

3. indigenous: native

4. romanticize: to think in a romantic way

5. modernist: modern

6. represses: holds back; suppresses

7. avenues: means of access

8. endeavor: activity; enterprise

9. contemporary: modern day

10. commerce: intellectual exchange or social interaction

11. pathological: habitual and compulsive; abnormal

LEARN MORE ABOUT VOCABULARY IN CONTEXT by visiting the following Web sites:

1. Vocabulary in Context Tutorial
   http://www3.cerritos.edu/reading/com

2. Word Games
   http://www.m-w.com/game/

3. Vocabulary Quizzes
   http://webster.commnet.edu/grammar/vocabulary.htm#quizzes

PART THREE

Using Word Parts to Expand Your Vocabulary

SECTION A Word Parts: The Bargain Table
for Vocabulary Building

Take your pick.

A. Study one word and learn one meaning.

B. Study one prefix (word beginning) and learn the meaning of over 100
   words.

No doubt you picked choice B, which describes a method of building your
vocabulary by learning word parts, the subject of this part of the text.

If you study the meaning of the word *pseudonym*, you end up knowing one
meaning (false name). If you study the prefix *pseudo-* (which means *false*) you
might be able to figure out nearly 400 words that begin with that prefix (*pseudo-
science, pseudonym, pseudobiological,* and so forth). The prefix *extra-* is used in
approximately 225 words. The root *dict-* unlocks the meaning of over 175 words;
the root *spec-* is the key to over 300 words.

By learning common beginnings, middles, and endings of words, called
word parts, you unlock the meaning of many more words than you would by
studying single meanings. Learning word parts is the bargain table of vocabulary
building. On a bargain table, you buy merchandise for less than you would nor-
mally expect to pay. On the word parts bargain table, you learn many more
words than you would expect for the cost (your time).

A letter or letters added to the beginning of a root is called a **prefix**.

Prefix + Root	Word
inter + change	interchange
mis + inform	misinform
trans + port	transport

A letter or letters added to the end of a root is called a **suffix**.

Root + Suffix	Word
sleep + y	sleepy
adopt + ion	adoption
normal + ly	normally

A **root** is a syllable, syllables, or an independent word that carries the basic
meaning of the word.

	Roots	Words Formed from Roots
Single Syllable	path, graph, cred	sympathy, graphic, credible
Multiple Syllables	ortho, astro, photo	orthopedics, astronaut, photograph
Whole Words	light, advantage, heart	lightness, advantageous, heartless

Roots are the basic building blocks upon which other words, sometimes called variations or derivatives, are formed. Some roots are formed from Latin or Greek words. For example, the Latin root *-fid* (which means faith) is used to form words such as *fidelity* (faithfulness), *infidel* (a person who is not faithful), and *confidence* (having faith in yourself). Whole-word roots are found in the dictionary under their own entries. (Whole-word roots are sometimes called base words.) For example, the word *excite* is a root word. The word *excitable* is not. It is formed from the root word *excite*.

Here are a few things you need to know about prefixes, suffixes, and roots.

1. Every word is built upon at least one root.

2. Words can have more than one prefix, root, or suffix.
   - Some words have two roots (*photo/graph*).
   - Some words have two prefixes (*un/sub/stantial*).
   - Some words have two suffixes (*beauti/ful/ly*)

3. Not all words have a prefix and a suffix.
   - Some words have neither a prefix nor a suffix (*train*).
   - Others have a suffix, but no prefix (*train/able*).
   - Others have a prefix but no suffix (*un/train*).

4. The spelling of prefixes and roots may change when they are combined with other word parts. For example, the prefix *com-* (meaning together) changes when combined with the root that follows it. The prefix *com-* along with the root word *relate* combines and changes spelling to form the word *correlate* (to show or establish a connection or relationship).

5. Sometimes you may identify a group of letters as a prefix or root, but find that it does not carry the meaning of the prefix or root. For example, the first three letters in the word *missile* are part of the root and are not the prefix *mis-*, which means wrong or bad.

EXERCISE 3-1

Locate the whole word that functions as the root of each of the following boldfaced words. Write the root word and the meaning of the boldfaced word in the space provided.

EXAMPLE: The **generosity** of the city's restaurant owners was evident; the shelves of the food pantry were well-stocked.

generous; willingness to give

1. If you are color-blind, you cannot **differentiate** between shades of blue.

   differ; to perceive a difference

2. Many Americans are guilty of conspicuous **consumption**.

   consume; the using up of goods and services by consumer purchasing

3. The title of the sculpture was accompanied by an **explanatory** note in the program.

   explain; serving or intended to explain

4. The **likelihood** of my getting an A in the class seemed remote after the last exam.

   likely; probability

5. The judge pronounced sentence on the convicted killer **dispassionately**.

   passion; unaffected by passion, emotion, or bias

6. We thought her remarks at the rally were **inflammatory** and uncalled for.

   flame; arousing strong emotion, especially anger, belligerence, or desire

7. The **righteousness** of their crusade was never in doubt.

   right; moral justification

8. The gentleman on my right at the dinner party was an **insufferable** bore!

   suffer; intolerable

9. Several weightlifters were **disqualified** from the competition for having used steroids.

   qualify; declared ineligible

10. Our **unsteadiness** on land was caused by a rough crossing on the ferry.

    steady; unstability, wavering

SECTION B Word Parts and Academic Disciplines

You are taking a human anatomy and physiology course, and you have hundreds of new terms to learn. You must learn names of muscles, joints, and nerves, not to mention the names of the 206 bones in the body. Learning all these words one by one would be a formidable task. One way to survive in courses such as these is to learn prefixes, roots, and suffixes that will enable you to figure out many word meanings, rather than to memorize their individual meanings.

Each academic discipline, and especially the sciences, use prefixes, roots, and suffixes as language building blocks. You can learn sets or groups of words with similar prefixes or roots. Here are a few common prefixes and roots used in medical, legal, and biological fields, along with a sampling of the words you can figure out based on them.

Common Prefixes and Roots		Words Using These Word Parts
Medicine	*derma-* (skin)	dermatologist, dermatitis
	-itis (inflammation of)	dermatitis, appendicitis
	cardio- (heart)	cardiac, cardiography, cardiogram
	pod(o)- (foot)	podiatrist, podogram, pododynia
Biology	*-osis* (condition or process)	symbiosis
	photo- (light)	photosynthesis
	cyto- (study of cells)	cytoplasm
	exo- (outside)	exoskeleton
Law	*feder-* (treaty, league)	federal, federation
	judic- (judgment)	judicial, adjudicant
	jur(is)- (law, right)	jury, justice
	leg(is)- (law, contract)	legislation, legal

Some students find it helpful to create an index card file or computer file of important prefixes, roots, and suffixes. You can devise creative ways of organizing your files, depending on the discipline you are studying. For example, for an anatomy and physiology course, one student color-coded her index cards to correspond to various systems of the body.

SECTION C   Prefixes: Beginnings that Change Word Meanings

Some words use the same root words, but due to the prefixes that have been added, carry very different meanings—for example, important–unimportant; usual–unusual; pro-choice–anti-choice. Prefixes are powerful tools to adapt and change word meanings. They will unlock the meaning of thousands of words and can make a dramatic difference in your vocabulary.

Not all prefixes create opposite meanings as those shown above. Prefixes can suggest negatives ("not"), or they can suggest quantities. They can also suggest direction, location, or placement. Some prefixes indicate particular fields of study as well.

Prefixes Meaning "Not" (Negative or Opposite)

Table 3-1 lists common prefixes that may suggest negative or opposite meanings than the root on which they are based. The prefix *ir-* added to the word *responsible* forms the word *irresponsible* (not responsible).

One factor that makes prefixes tricky to work with is knowing which prefix to add to which root word. For example, if you want to add a prefix meaning *not* to the base word *conclusive*, which of the prefixes meaning *not* should you add, *un-*, *in-*, or *non-?* Unfortunately, there is no easy answer. The right answer is to add the prefix *in-*, forming the word *inconclusive*. *Nonconclusive* and *unconclusive* are not words. In these situations, there is usually no rule to follow. Instead, you should

TABLE 3-1   Common Prefixes Meaning "Not" (Negative)

Prefix	Meaning	Sample Word
a-	not	asymmetrical
anti-	against	antiwar
contra-	against, opposite	contradict
dis-	part, away, not	disagree
in/il/ir/im-	not	incorrect/illogical/irreversible/impossible
mal-	bad, wrong	malpractice
mis-	wrongly	misunderstand
non-	not	nonfiction
un-	not	unpopular
pseudo-	false	pseudoscientific

check your dictionary to be sure that you have combined a prefix and root or base word correctly to form a real word.

The prefixes *il-*, *im-*, and *ir-*, all of which do mean *not*, are a special case. Which to use depends on the sound of the letter that follows the prefix. The prefix *il-* is added to words that begin with the letter *l* (*illegal*). The prefix *im-* is added to words that begin with the letters *b, m,* or *p* (*imbalance, immobile, impossible*). The prefix *ir-* is added to words that begin with the letter *r*.

EXERCISE 3-2

For each boldfaced word in the following sentences, underline the prefix and write the meaning of the word in the space provided.

EXAMPLE: Be sure to use **nonsexist** language.

not discriminating on the basis of gender

1. Because my daughter's handwriting is nearly **illegible**, she got a D on her report card for handwriting.

   unreadable

2. When we found the kitten, it was suffering from **malnutrition.**

   poor nutrition

3. Samuel Clemens wrote books under the **pseudonym** Mark Twain.

   false name

4. The diagnosis was difficult to make because the patient's symptoms were **atypical.**

   not typical or usual

5. It was **imprudent** of him to spend his last dollar on a lottery ticket.

   not wise

6. The city councilman was accused of **misallocating** funds.

   improperly assigning

7. The earthquake **dislodged** several large boulders on the mountain.

   forced out of place

8. His high blood pressure was a **contraindication** for surgery at this time.

   condition that makes treatment inadvisable

9. The country maintained a policy of **nonaggression** toward its neighbors.

   no attacks

10. It was **demoralizing** to lose the game after having been ahead by ten runs.

    disappointing

For each of the following words, add a prefix to form a word opposite in meaning to the word given. Check a dictionary if you are unsure of which prefix to add.

EXAMPLE: trust _____distrust; mistrust_____

1. religious _____irreligious_____
2. conscious _____unconscious_____
3. perfect _____imperfect_____
4. familiar _____unfamiliar_____
5. social _____antisocial, unsocial, asocial_____

6. belief _____disbelief, unbelief_____
7. nutrition _____malnutrition_____
8. moral _____immoral, amoral_____
9. compliant _____noncompliant_____
10. liberal _____illiberal_____

For each of the following sentences, circle the letter of the choice that best explains the meaning of the boldfaced word. Use your knowledge of prefixes and a dictionary if necessary.

1. The counselor helped the teenager **redefine** her goals.
   a. explain
   b. state over again
   c. defend
   d. manage

2. It was obvious that the mayor was **unacquainted** with the plight of immigrants in the city.
   a. familiar
   b. unexperienced
   c. not knowledgeable about
   d. not concerned about

3. Due to the group's radical position on animal rights, Janine **disaffiliated** herself with the Rights for Animals Association.
   a. remove from involvement
   b. remain partially involved
   c. maintain several associations
   d. carry a false association

4. We were **misinformed** about the store's hours.
   a. distracted
   b. given incorrect information
   c. directed accurately
   d. displeased

5. Our waiter laughingly tried to convince us that the triple chocolate cake was **noncaloric.**
   a. fat free
   b. not caffeinated
   c. nutritious
   d. having few or no calories

6. The federal official was charged with **misappropriation** of funds.
   a. take wrongly
   b. receive lawfully
   c. benefit
   d. encourage

7. After being sprayed by a skunk, our **malodorous** dog hid under the porch.
   a. naughty
   b. unhappy
   c. bad-smelling
   d. ill

8. The child's behavior was **unpredictable.**

   a. as expected

   b. outrageous

   c. obviously aggressive

   (d.) difficult to foretell

9. The weather forecaster said that travel through the mountains was **inadvisable.**

   a. forbidden

   (b.) not wise

   c. impossible

   d. encouraged

10. The talk show host was known for his **irreverent** sense of humor.

   a. bizarre

   b. dignified

   (c.) disrespectful

   d. unbiased

Prefixes Referring to Number or Amount

Some prefixes, when added to a root, suggest number or amount. The prefix *semi-* means *half*. A *semicircle*, then, is a half circle. Table 3-2 on page 52 lists common prefixes that refer to number or amount.

EXERCISE 3-5

Match the prefix in column A with its meaning in column B. Write your answer in the space provided.

	Column A		Column B
1. __e__	semi	a.	three
2. __l__	micro	b.	ten
3. __i__	centi	c.	two
4. __j__	quad	d.	five
5. __a__	tri	e.	half
6. __k__	equi	f.	thousand
7. __c__	bi/di/du	g.	many
8. __d__	quint/pent	h.	one
9. __g__	multi/poly	i.	hundred
10. __f__	milli	j.	four
11. __b__	deci	k.	equal
12. __h__	mono/uni	l.	small

TABLE 3-2 Prefixes: Number or Amount

Prefix	Meaning	Sample Word
mono/uni-	one	monocle/unicycle
bi/di/du-	two	bimonthly/divorce/duet
tri-	three	triangle
quad-	four	quadrant
quint/pent-	five	quintet/pentagon
deci-	ten	decimal
centi-	hundred	centigrade
milli-	thousand	milligram
micro-	small	microscope
multi/poly-	many	multipurpose/polygon
semi-	half	semicircle
equi-	equal	equidistant

EXERCISE 3-6

Supply a word that completes the meaning of each of the following sentences.

EXAMPLE: A **pentagon** has _____five_____ sides.

1. A **multilingual** person can speak _____many_____ languages.

2. A **bicentennial** celebration occurs every _____two hundred_____ years.

3. A **milliliter** is equal to _____one-thousandth_____ of a liter.

4. A **decapod** is a crustacean with _____ten_____ legs.

5. A **pentathlon** is an athletic contest in which each participant competes in _____five_____ track and field events.

6. **Monosyllabic** words have _____one_____ syllable(s).

7. The trillium is considered a **trifoliate** flower because it has _____three_____ leaves.

8. An **equilateral** geometric figure has _____equal_____ sides.

9. A **duologue** is a conversation between _____two_____ people.

10. A **semiannual** publication is issued _____twice_____ a year.

Prefixes Suggesting Direction, Location, or Placement

Some prefixes suggest direction, location, or placement. For example, the prefix *post-* means *after*, and *postoperative care* refers to care given after (direction in time) an operation. Table 3-3 lists common prefixes that refer to direction, location or placement.

TABLE 3-3 Prefixes: Direction, Location, or Placement

Prefix	Meaning	Sample Word
ab-	away	absent
ad-	toward	adhesive
ante/pre-	before	antecedent/premarital
circum/peri-	around	circumference/perimeter
com/col/con-	with, together	compile/collide/convene
de-	away, from	depart
dia-	through	diameter
ex/extra-	from, out of, former	extramarital/ex-wife
hyper-	over, excessive	hyperactive
inter-	between	interpersonal
intro/intra-	within, into, in	introduction
peri-	around	perimeter
post-	after	posttest
re-	back, again	review
retro-	backward	retrospect
sub-	under, below	submarine
super-	above, extra	supercharge
tele-	far	telescope
trans-	across, over	transcontinental

EXERCISE 3-7

Match the prefix in column A with its meaning in column B. Write your answer in the space provided.

	Column A		Column B
1. __j__	con	a.	back, again
2. __c__	super	b.	before
3. __h__	retro	c.	above, extra
4. __f__	ad	d.	away, from
5. __e__	intro/intra	e.	within, into, in
6. __d__	de	f.	toward
7. __a__	re	g.	across
8. __g__	trans	h.	backward
9. __b__	ante/pre	i.	around
10. __i__	peri	j.	with, together

EXERCISE 3-8

Match the prefix in column A with its meaning in column B. Write your answer in the space provided.

Column A

1. __a__ inter
2. __h__ hyper
3. __d__ ex
4. __e__ dia
5. __j__ circum
6. __f__ com
7. __b__ tele
8. __i__ ab
9. __c__ sub
10. __g__ post

Column B

a. between
b. far
c. under, below
d. from, out of, former
e. through
f. with, together
g. after
h. over, excessive
i. away
j. around

EXERCISE 3-9

Circle the choice that completes the meaning of each of the following sentences.

1. A **hyperactive** child has _____ energy.
   a. too little
   b. too much
   c. unsupervised
   d. over directed

2. A **periotic** device is one that is situated _____ the ear.
   a. around
   b. on
   c. in
   d. opposite

3. An **antebellum** mansion is one that was built _____ the Civil War.
   a. before
   b. during
   c. after
   d. as a result of

4. The **diameter** of a circle is the distance _____ the circle.
   a. around
   b. over
   c. under
   d. through

5. A **retrorocket** on a missile is used to _____ the motion of the missile.
   a. speed up
   b. reverse
   c. alter the direction
   d. accelerate

6. A **telephoto** lens on a camera allows you to photograph _____ objects.
   a. moving
   b. distant
   c. close-up
   d. stationary

7. **Extraterritorial** waters are those located _____ territorial boundaries.

   a. within

   b. below

   (c.) outside

   d. above

8. A musical **interlude** is a short piece inserted _____ the parts of a longer composition.

   a. before

   b. after

   (c.) between

   d. during

9. A thief who **absconds** with the money has _____.

   a. surrendered/given in

   b. returned

   c. been caught

   (d.) gone away

10. A **transdermal** patch works by supplying medication _____.

   (a.) across or through the skin

   b. only on the surface of the skin

   c. orally

   d. into veins

Prefixes Referring to Fields of Study

Other prefixes refer to particular fields of study or particular disciplines, as well as suggest other related meanings. The prefix *bio-* means *life*, and *biology* is the study of life. Related words also use the prefix. *Biopsy* means a sample of tissue removed from a *living body* for examination or study. A *biography* is the story of a person's *life*. Table 3-4 lists common prefixes that refer to fields of study.

TABLE 3-4   Prefixes: Fields of Study

Prefix	Meaning	Sample Word
anthropo-	human being	anthropology, anthropomorphic
archaeo-	ancient	archaeology, archaic
bio-	life	biology, biotechnology
geo-	earth	geology, geography
gyneco-	woman	gynecology, gynecopathy
pysch-	mind	psychology, psychopath
theo-	God or gods	theology, theologian

EXERCISE 3-10

Underline the correct answer of the two given in parentheses.

1. A **biographer** is one who writes the story of (a fictional event, <u>a person's life</u>).

2. An **archaeopteryx** is (<u>an ancient</u>, a wild) bird.

3. **Theomorphism** is the depiction of human beings as having the form of (an animal, <u>a god</u>).

4. A **gynecocracy** is a society or government ruled by (men, <u>women</u>).

5. An **anthropocentric** person regards (<u>human beings</u>, plant life) as the central element of the universe.

6. A person suffering from **psychosis** has a severe (<u>mental</u>, physical) disorder.

7. A **bioastronaut** is concerned with the effects of space flight on (the solar system, <u>living organisms</u>).

8. **Geothermal** temperatures relate to the internal heat of the (<u>earth</u>, sun).

9. A **psychosurgeon** performs surgery to correct severe (<u>mental</u>, breathing) disorders.

10. If a law is considered **archaic**, it is (modern, <u>out-of-date</u>).

EXERCISE 3-11

Circle the choice that best states the meaning of each of the following boldfaced words.

1. Many people are switching to **decaffeinated** coffee.
   a. strong
   b. weak
   (c.) caffeine free
   d. caffeine added

2. The will was **uncontested.**
   a. debated
   (b.) not challenged
   c. not resolved
   d. hostile

3. It was difficult to find an **impartial** judge for the talent contest.
   (a.) not biased
   b. unrelated
   c. sympathetic
   d. qualified

4. Their nightly routine included a **postprandial** walk around the neighborhood.
   a. before dinner
   b. before dessert
   (c.) after dinner
   d. before bed

5. The patient received **intramuscular** injections of cortisone to reduce the swelling.
   a. between muscles
   (b.) into the muscle
   c. away from the muscle
   d. under the muscle

6. The space shuttle made a **circumlunar** voyage.
   a. away from the moon
   b. beyond the moon
   c. to the moon
   (d.) around the moon

7. She was **hypersensitive** about her cooking ability.
   (a.) overly sensitive
   b. unaffected
   c. unconcerned
   d. confident

8. Anders was much more **introverted** than his sisters.
   a. outgoing
   b. entertaining
   (c.) shy
   d. active

9. All members are expected to **adhere** to club rules.

    a. create   c. defend

    (b.) follow or abide by   d. ignore

10. Our ficus tree **defoliates** whenever we move it to another room.

    a. blooms   c. dries up

    b. shows new growth   (d.) loses leaves

EXERCISE 3-12

There are many more prefixes than those listed in Tables 3-1, 3-2, 3-3, and 3-4. Use a desk dictionary to locate and write the meaning of each of the following prefixes. Then write two words using each prefix and use one in a sentence.   Answers will vary.

EXAMPLE: *ambi-*   around, both; ambisexual, ambivalent

                   My parents were ambivalent about their decision to sell their house.

1. *anti-*   against; antibacterial, antidepressant

2. *chrono-*   time; chronological, chronicle

3. *co-*   together; cohabitation, coworkers

4. *lacto-*   milk; lactate, lactose, lactoprotein

5. *hetero-*   different; heterosexual, heterogeneous

6. *homo-*   same; homosexual, homgeneous

7. *hydro-*   water; hydroelectric, hydroplane

8. *idio-*   one's own; idiom, idiosyncratic

9. *patho-*   disease, suffering; pathology, pathogen

10. *ultra-*   beyond, excessive; ultraconservative, ultralight

Read the following paragraphs and use your knowledge of prefixes to identify the meaning of each of the words in bold-faced type. Use a dictionary if necessary.

A. How can we **reconcile** such **contradictory** conclusions about heroin addiction? Certainly William Burroughs' description of his own addiction to heroin (and similar reports by others) is accurate. He did not make it up. At the same time, Johnson and his associates are also accurate. They did not make up their findings either. And other researchers have noted that some people use heroin on an **irregular** basis, such as at weekend parties, without becoming addicted. Where does this leave us? From the mixed reports, it seems reasonable to conclude that heroin is addicting to some people, but not to others. Some people do become addicts and match the **stereotypical** profile. Others use heroin on a recreational basis. Both, then, maybe right. With the evidence we have at this point, it would be **inappropriate** to side with either extreme.

Adapted from Henslin, *Social Problems*, Sixth Edition, p. 118

1. Reconcile   to make compatible or consistent
2. Contradictory   situation in which two or more ideas are opposite or inconsistent
3. Irregular   not regular
4. Stereotypical   following a set image or type
5. Inappropriate   not suitable

B. Why are there such **unaccounted** for differences in promiscuity and commitment between male and female **homosexuals**? Some would argue that the chief reason can be traced to differences in their socialization. Girls are more likely to associate sex with emotional relationships, and, like their **heterosexual** counterparts, lesbians tend to conform to this basic expectation. Similarly, boys tend to learn to separate sex from affection, to validate their **self-images**, by how much sex they have, and to see fidelity as a restriction on their **independence**.

Adapted from Henslin, *Social Problems*, Sixth Edition, p. 72

1. Unaccounted   not explained
2. Homosexuals   individuals attracted to those of the same sex
3. Heterosexual   individuals attracted to those of the opposite sex
4. Self-images   concepts of ones selves
5. Independence   freedom, not dependent

C. An especially **unstable** class of molecules are oxygen free radicals, sometimes just called free radicals. Some free radicals are accidentally produced in small amounts during the normal process of energy transfer within living cells. Exposure to chemicals, radiation, **ultraviolet** light, cigarette smoke, and air pollution may also create free radicals. We now know that certain enzymes and nutrients called **antioxidants** are the body's natural defense against oxygen free radicals. Antioxidants may prevent oxidation by **inactivating** them quickly before they can damage other molecules. Many health experts believe that antioxidant vitamins reduce the chance of certain cancers and the risk of **cardiovascular** death.

Adapted from Michael D. Johnson, *Human Biology*, Second Edition, p. 27

1. Unstable   <u>not steady, easily changed</u>

2. Ultraviolet   <u>rays beyond violet in the visible spectrum</u>

3. Antioxidants   <u>substances that prevent or inhibit oxidation</u>

4. Inactivating   <u>not functioning normally</u>

5. Cardiovascular   <u>pertaining to the heart and blood vessels</u>

SECTION D   Roots: The Building Blocks of Language

Did you know that . . .

- **The word *automatic*, as in *automatic transmission*, comes from the ancient Greek word *automatos* which means self-acting? (Wouldn't the ancient Greeks who traveled on foot be pleased to know they helped name a part of modern automobiles?)**

- **The word *hamburger* may have originated in Hamburg, Germany, where pounded beef steak was served.**

- **The word *dandelion* is borrowed from an Old French word meaning "tooth of the lion," referring to the sharp leaves of the plant.**

Roots are the building blocks of our language. Every word has at least one. Some roots, such as *dict-* and *spec-*, are used in hundreds of English words. By learning the meaning of common root words, you will have the key to thousands of previously unknown words. There are hundreds of roots that are not whole words. They form the basis for thousands of words. It is important to know that the spelling of roots can change as they are combined with other roots. Often the spelling of the root changes to make pronunciation of the newly formed word easier.

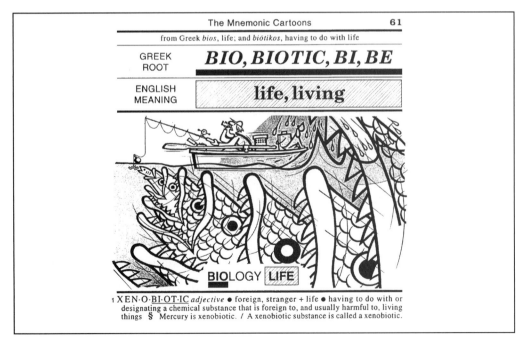

FIGURE 3-1

Ten Useful Roots

This section contains an extensive review of ten of the most useful roots.

1. *cap-* **(take, hold):** Someone who is **captured** is taken away or held. **Capacity** is the amount something can hold.

   captivate (verb): To hold one's attention.
   > The six-year-old was **captivated by** *Sesame Street*.

   captor (noun): One who holds.
   > The **captor** treated his prisoners well.

   capacious (adjective): Capable of holding a large amount, roomy.
   > The hotel room was surprisingly **capacious.**

2. *-cede* **(go):** To **precede** is to go before. To **secede** is to withdraw or go away from.

   exceed (verb): To go beyond.
   > The Broadway show **exceeded** our expectations.

   intercede (verb): To go between.
   > The attorney **interceded** in the argument between the divorced couple.

   proceed (verb): To go forward.
   > The couple decided to **proceed** with their plans for divorce.

   recede (verb): To go back.
   > The flood waters finally **receded.**

3. *cred-* **(trust or believe):** Someone who is **credible** is believable. **Credentials** are records that cause others to believe in someone.

   credit (noun): Trust, as in financial trust.
   > It is wise to check your **credit** rating.

   credulous (adjective): Gullible, believing too readily.
   > She was **credulous** enough to believe she would win the sweepstakes.

   incredible (adjective): Beyond belief, implausible, not easy to believe.
   > Teachers hear some **incredible** explanations from their students about missing or incomplete homework.

4. *dict-* **(tell, say):** A **dictionary** tells what words mean. In a **dictatorship**, the ruler has final say. In English words, the spelling may change to *dic-* or *dit-*.

   contradict (verb): To say the opposite.
   > The child **contradicted** her parents.

   dictate (verb): To express orally to another person, to command.
   > The manager **dictated** the new accounting procedures to the staff.

   dictatorial (adjective): Exercising excessive power or authority.
   > The nursery school teacher seemed **dictatorial** when she told students how to play the game.

   diction (noun): Wording, use of words in speech and writing.
   > Ellen was given a C for the poor **diction** in her essay.

5. *mis-/mit-* **(send):** A **message** is something that is sent to someone. To **omit** something is to leave out (send it away).

   intermittent (adjective): coming and going at intervals (To send at intervals).
   > The rain was **intermittent.**

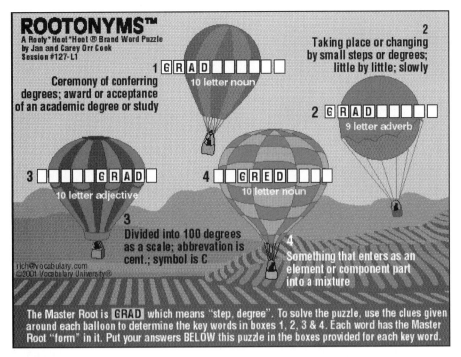

FIGURE 3-2

Hints:

- Answer 1: GRAD—step, walk, degree—Keyword is 10 letter noun—Ceremony of conferring degrees; award or acceptance of an academic degree or study.
- Answer 2: GRAD—step, walk, degree—Keyword is 9 letter adverb—Taking place or changing by small steps or degrees; little by little; slowly.
- Answer 3: GRAD—step, walk, degree—Keyword is 10 letter adjective—Divided into 100 degrees as a scale; abbreviation is cent.; symbol is C.
- Answer 4: GRED—step, walk, degree—Keyword is 10 letter noun—Something that enters as an element or component part into a mixture.

---

missile (noun): A weapon fired (sent) toward a target.
The **missile** struck the village.

promise (verb): To send forth, to indicate what might be expected.
He **promised** us that the check was in the mail.

transmit (verb): To send across a distance.
The message was **transmitted** overseas.

6. *port-* **(carry):** Something that is **portable** can be carried. To **transport** something is to carry it across a distance.

portend (verb): To carry a warning.
Those dark clouds in the east **portend** a storm.

porter (noun): One who carries something.
The **porter** delivered the bags to our hotel room.

portfolio (noun): A case for carrying a document.
Kerry brought his **portfolio** of drawings to the interview.

portly (adjective): To carry weight, stocky.
The **portly** man had trouble getting into his seat on the airplane.

7. *sen-* (**feel**): Someone who is **sensitive** to criticism feels or is affected by it. **Sensory** organs allow us to feel and experience our environment.

senseless (adjective): Unconscious, lacking feeling.
    The destruction of our neighbor's mailbox was a **senseless** crime.

sensibility (noun): Mental receptivity, capacity for refined feelings.
    A musician's **sensibility** to pitch and tone is essential when composing music.

sensor (noun): Device that responds (senses) a physical event.
    Our skin serves as a **sensor** for heat, cold, pressure, touch, and pain.

sentimental (adjective): Having tender feelings or emotions.
    The wedding photos made my grandmother **sentimental.**

8. *spec-/spect-* (**look, see**): **Spectacles** are eyeglasses that enable one to see. A **spectacle** is a public performance or display, often of bad behavior.

inspect (verb): To look closely, to examine critically.
    The customs agent **inspected** our passports.

spectator (noun): One who views, onlooker, witness.
    One thousand **spectators** attended the stadium's opening ceremony.

retrospect (noun): The act of looking backwards or thinking about the past.
    In **retrospect**, I realize I made the wrong decision.

perspective (noun): Point of view, the relative position of object or events.
    From my **perspective**, the crowd appeared unruly and threatening.

9. *sym-/syn-* (**same, together**): A **symphony** orchestra plays together. **Synonyms** have similar meanings.

symbiosis (noun): The living together of different species of organisms.
    A kind of **symbiosis** exists between a parasite and its host.

symmetry (noun): Regularity (sameness) in form.
    Pansies are characterized by the **symmetry** of their petals.

syndrome (noun): A set of symptoms that suggest a disease.
    She suffered from chronic fatigue **syndrome.**

synthesis (noun): Combination of elements into a whole.
    The project was a **synthesis** of several architects' work.

10. *voc-/vok-* (**call**): Think of a **vocation** as a calling. To **revoke** is to call back. (His driver's license was revoked.) Something that is **irrevocable** cannot be called back.

advocate (verb): A person who pleads in another's behalf.
    The governor appointed a former social worker as the chief child **advocate** for the state.

avocation (noun): A calling away, a hobby or special interest.
    Horseback riding has become my **avocation.**

evoke (verb): To call out, to draw out.
    The campfire **evoked** pleasant childhood memories.

provoke (verb): To call forth, to bring about, to cause anger.
    Witnesses report that the football player **provoked** the crowd to jeer.

EXPLORING LANGUAGE: Abbreviations and Acronyms—Shortcuts for Words and Phrases

Sarah wants to finish her <u>MBA</u> <u>asap</u> so she can apply for a job with an <u>ISP</u>; she plans to work her way up to becoming a <u>CEO</u>.

Each of the underlined words is an abbreviation; it is formed from the initial letters of a name of a series of words. *MBA* stands for <u>M</u>aster's of <u>B</u>usiness <u>A</u>dministration, *asap* means <u>a</u>s <u>s</u>oon <u>a</u>s <u>p</u>ossible, an *ISP* is an <u>I</u>nternet <u>s</u>ervice <u>p</u>rovider, and a *CEO* is a <u>c</u>hief <u>e</u>xecutive <u>o</u>fficer. Unlike an abbreviation, an acronym forms a word that has come into common usage. For example, the word *sonar* was formed from the words <u>so</u>und <u>n</u>avigation <u>r</u>anging.

   Use a dictionary or an Internet search to discover what each of the following acronyms or abbreviations stands for.

1. scuba   self contained underwater breathing apparatus
2. laser   light amplification (by) stimulated emission of radiation
3. radar   radio detecting and ranging
4. NASA   National Aeronautics and Space Administration

EXERCISE 3-14

Match the root in column A with its meaning in column B. Write your answer in the space provided.

	Column A		Column B
1. __h__	sym/syn	a.	take, hold
2. __g__	dict	b.	trust, believe
3. __j__	cede	c.	feel
4. __i__	mis/mit	d.	look, see
5. __c__	sen	e.	carry
6. __f__	voc/vok	f.	call
7. __a__	cap	g.	tell, say
8. __d__	spec/spect	h.	same, together
9. __e__	port	i.	send
10. __b__	cred	j.	go

From the list of words below, choose a word that fits the context of each of the following sentences and write the word in the space provided.

synchronized	perspective	invoked	omitted	preceded	portable
sensitized	credibility	capacity	dictum	retrospect	

EXAMPLE: In _____retrospect_____, I realized that I should have offered my sister a loan.

1. From our _____perspective_____ on the top of the mountain, islands in the sea looked tiny and unoccupied.

2. The concert hall was filled to _____capacity_____.

3. The plot of the action movie strained the audience's _____credibility_____.

4. Before the race, we _____synchronized_____ our watches.

5. The company's CEO issued a _____dictum_____ that all purchases must be approved in advance.

6. She deliberately _____omitted_____ her maiden name from the application.

7. We couldn't believe they brought a _____portable_____ TV to the beach!

8. The witness _____invoked_____ the Fifth Amendment.

9. His experience in Honduras _____sensitized_____ him to the plight of poor people everywhere.

10. The minister typically _____preceded_____ each sermon with a moment of silence.

Twenty-Five Common Roots

Table 3-5 on page 65 lists many of the most common roots—those that will be most useful to you in figuring out unknown words. (*Note:* This table, along with the roots listed above, corresponds with the roots listed in the McWhorter Reading Series vocabulary chapters; see Table 3-6 on p. 67 for additional roots.)

From the list of words below, choose a word that fits the context of each of the following sentences and write the word in the space provided.

chronology	beneficence	mortality	aster	facilitates	corporal
loquacious	intense	advent	inscribed	captive	

EXAMPLE: The _____captive_____ panther paced around her cage.

1. The _____mortality_____ rate among infants is shockingly high among the rural poor.

2. The flower called _____aster_____ is so named because it is shaped like a star.

3. His parents do not believe in spanking or _____corporal_____ punishment of any kind.

4. The actor—who typically played the strong, silent type—was _____loquacious_____ in the interview.

5. An English professor _____facilitates_____ our book club discussions.

6. Trying to study while your neighbors give a party requires _____intense_____ concentration.

7. Mother Teresa was known around the world for her _____beneficence_____.

8. The book was even more valuable because it had been _____inscribed_____ by the author.

9. With the _____advent_____ of the Internet, our ways of viewing the world are changed forever.

10. The detective tried to determine the _____chronology_____ of events that led up to the crime.

TABLE 3-5 Twenty-Five Common Roots

Root	Meaning	Sample Word
aud/audit	hear	audible, audition
aster/astro	star	asteroid, astronaut
bene	good, well	benefit
bio	life	biology
chron(o)	time	chronology
corp	body	corpse
duc/duct	lead	introduce
fact/fac	make, do	factory
fid	trust	confident
graph	write	telegraph
geo	earth	geophysics
log/logo/logy	study, thought	psychology
loqu	speak	colloquial
mort/mor	die, death	immortal
path	feeling	sympathy
phono	sound, voice	telephone
photo	light	photosensitive
scrib/script	write	inscription
sen/sent	feel	insensitive
tend/tent/tens	stretch or strain	tension
terr/terre	land, earth	territory
theo	god	theology
ven/vent	come	convention
vert/vers	turn	invert
vis/vid	see	invisible/video

Using your knowledge of prefixes and roots, circle the choice that best states the meaning of each boldfaced word or phrase.

1. Scientists are searching for **extraterrestrial life.**
   a. life beyond the earth
   b. life beneath the earth's surface
   c. microscopic life
   d. underwater life

2. The defendant's reply to the prosecutor was **inaudible.**
   a. nonsense
   b. unmistakable
   c. impossible to hear
   d. difficult to see

3. His **infidelity** was a major factor in the divorce.
   a. unhappiness
   b. dishonesty
   c. bad temper
   d. unfaithfulness

4. The exterior of the building was **nondescript**, but the interior was filled with treasures.
   a. lacking distinctive qualities
   b. unusual
   c. unmarked
   d. covered with writing

5. His unethical behavior put his assistant in an **untenable** position.
   a. easier
   b. difficult to bear
   c. secretive
   d. excusable

6. The **biodiversity** in the Amazon rain forest is astounding.
   a. animals
   b. climate
   c. plants
   d. variety of life

7. The manuscript was **revised** several times prior to publication.
   a. written
   b. turned down
   c. corrected/improved
   d. printed

8. The developer had a reputation for trying to **circumvent** zoning restrictions.
   a. strictly follow
   b. go around
   c. understand and apply
   d. debate

9. The surface of the moon appears to be **abiotic.**
   a. absence of life
   b. life-sustaining
   c. unknown
   d. unseen

10. The children performed especially **euphonious** selections for the nursing home residents.
    a. complicated
    b. harsh-looking
    c. unrestrained
    d. pleasant-sounding

TABLE 3-6   Roots for Additional Study

Root	Meaning	Sample Word	Root	Meaning	Sample Word
am	love	amorous	*man*	hand	manual
ann	year	annual	*nat*	born	native
cord	heart	cordial`	*ped*	foot	podiatrist
cur	run	excursion	*pel*	drive	propel
dent	tooth	dentist	*pop*	people	populace
form	shape	transform	*rupt*	break	interrupt
ject	throw	reject	*sect*	cut	intersection
lab	work	laborer	*tract*	pull	attraction
liber	free	liberty	*vac*	empty	vacant
lust	shine	luster	*ver*	turn	inversion

Roots for Additional Study

Table 3-6 above presents an additional twenty roots that will help you expand your knowledge of word parts.

EXERCISE 3-18

Supply the missing word in each of the following sentences. Choose words from the list supplied below.

lusterless	bisected	manufactured	vacuous	laboriously	vacant
pedometer	recurring	cordate		projectiles	annuity

EXAMPLE: Although the apartment was _____vacant_____, the landlord claimed he had no time to repaint it.

1. Many household products are _____manufactured_____ in foreign countries.

2. We used a _____pedometer_____ to measure how far we went this morning.

3. Every April, Carlos receives a $500 _____annuity_____ from his uncle.

4. The small town was _____bisected_____ by the railroad tracks.

5. The _____vacuous_____ expression on her face revealed that she was not paying attention.

6. We carried stones _____laboriously_____ from the riverbed to the house.

7. The actor appeared in a _____recurring_____ role on the soap opera.

8. The lovely, _____cordate_____ leaves of the wild ginger make it an appealing ground cover.

9. The unpopular player had to duck several _____projectiles_____ as he ran onto the field.

10. The violinist blamed her _____lusterless_____ performance on jet lag.

Underline the correct answer of the two given in parentheses, based on the root of the boldface word.

1. Someone with a **morbid** sense of humor (never laughs, <u>laughs at gloomy things</u>).

2. A **chronoscope** measures (sound, <u>time</u>) intervals.

3. A person who wears **dentures** has false (<u>teeth</u>, hair).

4. **Astrophysicists** are primarily concerned with the physics or (<u>stars</u>, space).

5. Many modern **monotheistic** religions are based on the belief in one (<u>god</u>, prophet).

6. Your friend who likes to (laugh, <u>talk</u>) is in a state of **loquacity.**

7. If you can identify with another person's (<u>feelings</u>, situation), you are said to be **empathetic.**

8. When musicians are **inducted** into the Rock-n-Roll Hall of Fame, they are (<u>brought in</u>, invited) as members.

9. Dams **divert** water by forcing it to (stay back, <u>go in a new direction</u>).

10. After the (<u>birth</u>, death) of her son, she experienced **postnatal** depression.

For each boldfaced word in the following sentences, underline the root and write the meaning of the word in the space provided.

1. The view of the Olympic Mountains from Hurricane Ridge was **spectacular.**

   amazing

2. New arrivals to this country must follow certain procedures to avoid being **deported** to their homelands.

   sent away from a country

3. The new regulations **supersede** those put in place a decade ago.

   replace

4. The school board was **incredulous** of the allegations against a well-respected teacher.

   skeptical, unbelieving

5. Not even the most astute political observer could have **predicted** the unexpected election results.

   said ahead of time; foretold

6. When the city officials heard about the coming blizzard, they called for an early **dismissal** for all government employees.

   leaving

7. Since the new manager had once been a union worker, she **sympathized** with the plight of the workers under her supervision.

   understood, had a sensitivity toward

8. Now that Carmen decided to study biology, he had to learn the **vocabulary** of the field.

collection of words particular to an academic discipline; terminology

9. Many screenwriters study the lives of famous people looking for interesting stories to develop into **biopics.**

biographical movies

10. Some of the smaller candy companies still make their chocolates by hand in their **factories.**

places where goods are made

EXERCISE 3-21

There are many more roots than those listed in this chapter. For each of the following roots, several words are given that use that root. Look your words up in a desk dictionary to try to discover the meaning of the root. Write that meaning in the space provided.   Answers will vary.

EXAMPLE:	-spire	inspire, perspire, transpire	Root Meaning:	breathe
1.	-clude/-cluse	include, recluse, preclude	Root Meaning:	close
2.	-plic	explicit, implicate	Root Meaning:	fold
3.	-cite	excite, incite	Root Meaning:	put into motion
4.	-pos	deposit, disposable, impose	Root Meaning:	put
5.	-creas	increase, decrease	Root Meaning:	grow
6.	-volve	revolve, involve, evolve	Root Meaning:	roll, turn
7.	-mature	premature, immature	Root Meaning:	ripe
8.	-cept	accept, except, susceptible	Root Meaning:	take
9.	-press	compress, expression, depressed	Root Meaning:	press
10.	-fer	infer, defer, prefer	Root Meaning:	carry, bear

EXERCISE 3-22

Read each of the following paragraphs and use your knowledge of roots to determine the meaning of each of the words underlined. If you have difficulty, consult a dictionary.

A. Is it possible that humankind is now, at last, at the end of its ability to increase food supplies? The answer to this question is a cautious "probably not." If demographers are correct in their projections of Earth's future population, the population can be fed. Humankind has scarcely begun to maximize productivity with the best contemporary technology, and that leading technology has been applied to only a small portion of Earth. Spreading urbanization is replacing agriculture in many places, but more lands can still be farmed.

Bergman and Renwick, *Introduction to Geography,* Second Edition, p. 323

1. projections   estimates into the future

2. population   total number of inhabitants

3. humankind   the human race

4. productivity   ability to produce or create

5. urbanization   creation of a city-like environment

B. Many of the problems found in Mexico's <u>agricultural</u> economy can also be found in Africa. Landholding is often <u>communal</u>, so successful farmers cannot expand their productivity. Many African governments themselves hold ownership of agricultural land and lease it to farmers. In Zimbabwe, for example, the government <u>nationalized</u> numerous large white-owned private farms that were <u>exporting</u> food. The government <u>relocated</u> black settlers onto the properties but retained ownership, so the farmers cannot borrow to invest in increasing productivity.

Bergmann and Renwick, *Introduction to Geography*, Second Edition, p. 332

1. agricultural   the science of farming

2. communal   small community of common interests

3. nationalized   convert from private to government ownership

4. exporting   shipping goods out of the country

5. relocated   moved to a new place

C. No country is completely self-sufficient in food. Most countries both import and export food despite the fact that portions of their own populations are <u>undernourished.</u> This may be due to <u>injustice</u> or civil strife. Political <u>instability</u> contributes to hunger. Several African countries, for example are environmentally richly endowed, yet a great many of their people go hungry. Peter Rosset, director of the Institute for Food and Development Policy, wrote, "There is no relationship between the <u>prevalence</u> of hunger in a given country and its population. The world today produces more food per <u>inhabitant</u> than ever before."

Bergman and Renwick, *Introduction to Geography*, Second Edition, p. 329

1. undernourished   not given sufficient amount of food

2. injustice   a wrong, a violation of one's rights

3. instability   not constant; not reliable or dependable

4. prevalence   widely or commonly occurring

5. inhabitant   one who occupies an area

Suffixes: Endings that Change a Word's Part of Speech

Adapt is a verb meaning to change in order to fit a specific situation.

What word describes a person who can change easily?* _____

What word describes the ability to change easily?* _____

What word describes a change that has been made?* _____

Suffixes are word endings that change the part of speech of a word. For example, adding the suffix *-y* to the noun *cream* forms the adjective *creamy*. A change of meaning also occurs when the part of speech is changed. For example, *teach* (to instruct) is a verb; by adding the suffix *-able* the adjective *teachable* (able to be taught, capable of learning) is formed and carries a different meaning.

Often several different words can be formed from a single root word by adding different suffixes.

Root	Suffix	New Word
right	*-ly*	rightly
right	*-ful*	rightful
right	*-ist*	rightist
right	*-eous*	righteous

If you know the meaning of the root word and the ways in which different suffixes affect the meaning of the root word, you will be able to figure out a word's meaning when a suffix is added. A list of common suffixes and their meanings appears in Table 3-7 on page 72.

You can expand your vocabulary by learning the variations in meaning that occur when suffixes are added to words you already know. When you find a word that you do not know, look for the root. Then, using the sentence the word is in (its context; see Part 2), figure out what the word means with the suffix added. Occasionally you may find that the spelling of the root word has been changed. For instance, a final *e* may be dropped, a final consonant may be doubled, or a final *y* may be changed to *i*. Consider the possibility of such changes when trying to identify the root word. Here are some examples.

The article was a **compilation** of facts.

root + suffix

compil(e) + -ation = something that has been compiled, or put together into an orderly form

We were concerned with the **legality** of our decision to change addresses.

root + suffix

legal + -ity = pertaining to legal matters

Our college is one of the most **prestigious** in the state.

root + suffix

prestig(e) + -ious = having prestige or distinction

> ** Answers:* **adaptable, adaptability, adaptation.** *Adaptable* **is an adjective,** *adaptability* **and** *adaptation* **are nouns.**

TABLE 3-7   Common Suffixes

Suffix	Sample Word	Suffix	Sample Word
Suffixes that refer to a state, condition, or quality		Suffixes that mean "one who"	
		-an	Italian
-able	touchable	-ant	participant
-ance	assistance	-ee	referee
-ation	confrontation	-eer	engineer
-ence	reference	-ent	resident
-ible	tangible	-er	teacher
-ion	discussion	-ist	activist
-ity	superiority	-or	advisor
-ive	permissive		
-ment	amazement	Suffixes that mean "pertaining to or referring to"	
-ness	kindness		
-ous	jealous	-al	autumnal
-ty	loyalty	-ship	friendship
-y	creamy	-hood	brotherhood
		-ward	homeward

EXERCISE 3-23

For each suffix shown in Table 3-7, write another example of a word you know that has that suffix.   Answers will vary.

EXERCISE 3-24

For each of the words listed below, add a suffix so that the word will complete the sentence. Write the new word in the space provided. Check a dictionary if you are unsure of the spelling.

EXAMPLE: **sex:** _____Sexist_____ language should be avoided in both speech and writing.

1. **eat:** We did not realize that the plant was _____edible_____ until we tasted its delicious fruit.

2. **compete:** The gymnastics _____competition_____ was our favorite part of the Olympics.

3. **decide:** It was difficult to be _____decisive_____ in such a stressful situation.

4. **Portugal:** Our favorite restaurant specializes in _____Portuguese_____ food.

5. **active:** She gained fame as a civil rights _____activist_____ in the 1960s.

6. **parent:** _____Parenthood_____ is one of the most rewarding experiences in life.

7. **vaccine:** You must receive several different _____vaccinations_____ before your trip to Africa.

8. **member:** We inadvertently allowed our _____membership_____ to the botanical garden to lapse.

9. **drive:** The abandoned car did not appear _____drivable_____ so a tow truck was summoned.

10. **celebrate:** The girls waited at the airport for hours to catch a glimpse of their favorite _____celebrity_____ .

How Suffixes Change Parts of Speech

You need to know how to change a word's part of speech, especially when you are writing or speaking. For example, you may want to use a verb that means to divide something into groups or classes. The noun *class* can be converted to a verb by adding the suffix *-ify*, forming the word *classify*. Or you may want to find a noun that describes the condition of being an individual. You could add the suffix *-ism*, forming the word *individualism*. A list of suffixes divided according to the part of speech they form appears in Table 3-8 below.

TABLE 3-8   Adding Suffixes to Form New Parts of Speech

Suffix	Sample Word	Suffix	Sample Word
Suffixes Used to Form Verbs		**Suffixes Used to Form Nouns**	
-ate	motivate	*-ac*	insomniac
-ify	quantify	*-ance, -ancy*	pregnancy
-ize	customize	*-ary*	adversary
		-dom	kingdom
Suffix Used to Form Adverbs		*-ence*	independence
-ly	lively	*-er*	teacher
		-hood	parenthood
Suffixes Used to Form Adjectives		*-ion, -tion*	transaction
-able, -ible	touchable	*-ism*	tourism
-ac, -ic	psychic	*-ist*	activist
-al	minimal	*-ment*	employment
-ant	belligerent	*-ness*	kindness
-ary	contrary	*-ship*	friendship
-dom	freedom	*-ure*	tenure
-en	brazen		
-ful	faithful		
-ive	attentive		
-like	birdlike		
-ous, -ious	anxious		
-some	wholesome		
-y	cloudy		

From the list of words below, choose a word that fits the context of each of the following sentences and write the word in the space provided.

qualifications   preferential   occupational   preferable   predictions   predicament

variations   predictable   qualifier   occupant   variable

EXAMPLE: Before our marriage, we never anticipated the financial _____predicament_____ we would face.

1. I decided that electing to take a pass/fail grade was _____preferable_____ to withdrawing from sociology.

2. The study focused on _____variations_____ in color among parakeets.

3. After the food critic was recognized, he was given _____preferential_____ treatment by the restaurant staff.

4. Out of ten athletes from his country, Ian was the only _____qualifier_____ for the finals.

5. The _____occupational_____ hazards for coal miners are many.

6. Her _____qualifications_____ for the job were outstanding.

7. The reviewer said the movie was weighed down by poor acting and a _____predictable_____ plot.

8. The only _____variable_____ we couldn't control was the weather.

9. Most of the mail was addressed simply to _____occupant_____.

10. Stock analysts were unable to make any _____predictions_____ about the company's future success.

For each word below, underline the suffix and indicate what part of speech the word is, using both Tables 3-7 and 3-8 as applicable.

EXAMPLE: hard**ship**   ___noun, "pertaining to"___

1. act**or**   _____noun_____

2. Peace**ful**   _____adjective_____

3. employ**ee**   _____noun_____

4. admi**ssion**   _____noun_____

5. star**ry**   _____adjective_____

6. neighbor**hood**   _____noun_____

7. qual**ify**   _____verb_____

8. **happ**<u>ily</u> <u>   adverb   </u>

9. **tox**<u>ic</u> <u>   adjective   </u>

10. **veg**<u>an</u> <u>   noun   </u>

EXERCISE 3-27

Match the suffix in Column B to the word in Column A it can combine with to create the requested type of word. Write the new word in the blank.

EXAMPLE: Forms a noun:

    <u> B </u> king <u>   kingdom   </u>

    A. -ly

    B. -dom

    C. -like

Column A   **Column B**

Forms a verb:

  <u> F </u> 1. donor <u>   donate   </u>   A. -ent/-ant

Forms a noun: B. -ly

  <u> H </u> 2. harmony <u> harmonize </u>   C. -ism

  <u> J </u> 3. happy <u> happiness </u>   D. -ion, -tion

  <u> C </u> 4. fascist <u> fascism </u>   E. -ful

  <u> D </u> 5. designate <u> designation </u>   F. -ate

Forms an adjective: G. -able

  <u> A </u> 6. fervor <u> fervent </u>   H. -ize

  <u> E </u> 7. harm <u> harmful </u>   I. -ous, ious

  <u> G </u> 8. consider <u> considerable </u>   J. -ness

  <u> I </u> 9. vary <u> various </u>

Forms an adverb:

  <u> B </u> 10. quick <u> quickly </u>

EXERCISE 3-28

For each word, create at least two new words by adding or changing suffixes. Indicate the part of speech for each new word. (Answers will vary—some possibilities are provided.)

EXAMPLE: **fish:** <u>fishy (adj.), fishlike (adj.), fisher (noun)</u>

1. **might:** <u>mighty (adj.), mightily (adv.)</u>

2. **participation:** <u>participate (verb), participant (noun)</u>

3. **clear:** <u>clearly (adv.), clearance (noun), clarify (verb)</u>

4. **equal:** <u>equalize (verb), equally (adv.), equalizer (noun)</u>

5. **depend:** dependable (adj.), dependence (noun)

6. **tech:** technical (adj.), technic (adj.), technician (noun)

7. **prevent:** preventable (adj.), prevention (noun), preventer (noun)

8. **system:** systemic (adj.), systematic (adj.), systemize (verb)

9. **function:** functional (adj.), functionary (noun), functionless (adj.)

10. **relation:** relational (adj.), relationally (adj.), relationship (noun)

EXERCISE 3-29

Read the following paragraphs and use your knowledge of prefixes, roots, and suffixes to determine the meaning of the underlined words listed below.

A. <u>Professional</u> criminals make their <u>livelihood</u> from crime. They include not only the highly <u>romanticized</u> jewel thieves, <u>safecrackers,</u> and <u>counterfeiters</u>, but also professional shoplifters, pickpockets, and fences—those who buy stolen goods for resale. Their activities, although illegal, are a form of work, and they pride themselves on their skills and successes.

Henslin, Social Problems, Sixth Edition, p. 187

1. professional   engaged in a profession

2. livelihood   means or support, subsistence

3. romanticized   characteristic of romance; high level or interest and emotion

4. safecrackers   people who break into safes

5. counterfeiters   people who produce fake currency

B. Certain types of crime are easier to get away with than others. Running less risk are <u>political</u> criminals who attempt to maintain the status quo and white-collar criminals who commit crimes in the name of a <u>corporation</u>, and those who comprise the top levels of organized crime. <u>Respectability</u>, wealth, power, and underlings insulate them. Those in the second group are insulated by the corporation's desire to avoid negative <u>publicity</u>. Those who run the highest risk of arrest are "soldiers" at the lowest levels of organized crime, who are considered <u>expendable</u>.

Adapted from Henslin, Social Problems, Sixth Edition, p. 192

1. political   relating to the affairs of government

2. corporation   body legally recognized to conduct business

3. respectability   quality of being respected; regarded as worthy and proper

4. publicity   public interest and awareness

5. expendable   not worth saving; open to sacrifice

C. The proponents of capital punishment argue that it is an appropriate <u>retribution</u> for <u>heinous</u> crimes, that it deters, and, of course, that it is an effective <u>incapacitator</u>. Its critics argue that killing is never justified. Opponents also argue that the death penalty is <u>capricious</u>: Jurors deliberate in secrecy and indulge their prejudices in recommending death, and judges are <u>irrational</u>—merciful to some but not to others.

Adapted from Henslin, Social Problems, Sixth Edition, p. 205

1. retribution   punishment; something justly deserved

2. heinous   abominable, very wicked and hateful

3. incapacitator   something that deprives of strength or ability, disables

4. capricious   unpredictable, subject to whim

5. irrational   not logical

Applying and *Integrating* What You Have Learned

EXERCISE 3-30   APPLYING YOUR SKILLS IN PSYCHOLOGY

Read the following passage and use your knowledge of word parts and context to figure out the meaning of each boldfaced word. Write a synonym or definition in the space provided. Consult a dictionary if necessary.

Erik Erikson proposed that each individual must successfully **navigate** a series of psychosocial stages, each of which presented a particular conflict or crisis. Erikson identified eight stages in the life cycle. Each stage requires a new level of social interaction; success or failure in achieving it can change the course of **subsequent** development in a positive or negative direction.

In Erikson's first stage, an infant needs to develop a basic sense of trust in the environment through interaction with caregivers. Trust is a natural **accompaniment** to a strong attachment relationship with a parent who provides food, warmth, and the comfort of physical closeness. But a child whose basic needs are not met, who experiences **inconsistent** handling, lack of physical closeness and warmth, and the frequent absence of a caring adult, may develop a **pervasive** sense of mistrust, insecurity, and anxiety. This child will not be pre-

pared for the second stage, which requires the individual to be adventurous.

With the development of walking and the beginnings of language, there is an **expansion** of a child's exploration and **manipulation** of objects (and sometimes people). With these activities should come a comfortable sense of **autonomy** and of being a capable and worthy person. Excessive restriction or criticism at this second stage may lead instead to self-doubts, while demands beyond the child's ability can discourage the child's efforts to **persevere** in mastering new tasks. The 2-year-old who insists that a particular ritual be followed or demands the right to do something without help is acting out of a need to **affirm** his or her autonomy and adequacy.

—Adapted from Zimbardo and Gerrig, *Psychology and Life*, Fifteenth Edition, pp. 404–405.

1. navigate: move through

2. subsequent: following after, succeeding

3. accompaniment: complement, companion

4. inconsistent: not regular or predictable

5. pervasive: present throughout

6. expansion: opening up

7. manipulation: to operate using the hands

8. autonomy: independence

9. persevere   persist or remain constant in the face of difficulties

10. affirm: support or confirm

EXERCISE 3-31   APPLYING YOUR SKILLS IN INTERPERSONAL COMMUNICATION

Read the following passage and use your knowledge of word parts and context to figure out the meaning of each boldfaced word. Write a synonym or definition in the space provided. Consult a dictionary if necessary.

The most obvious yet elusive component of small group communication is the spoken word. Words lie at the very heart of who and what people are. Their ability to represent the world **symbolically** gives humans the **capacity** to foresee events, to reflect on past experiences, to plan, to make decisions, and to consciously control their own behavior. Words are the tools with which people make sense of the world and share that sense with others.

While words can **empower** people and can influence attitudes and behaviors, they can also **impede** a process. While speech communication gives individuals access to the ideas and inner worlds of other group members, it can also set up barriers to effective communication. Some more subtle but pervasive word barriers are (1) bypassing, (2) allness, and (3) fact-inference confusion.

Bypassing takes place when two people assign different meanings to the same word. In groups, the problem of bypassing is **compounded** by the number of people involved; the possibility for multiple misunderstandings is always present. To overcome word barriers, people must understand that words are subjective. They need to check that what they understand from others is really what those others intend.

Allness statements are simple but untrue **generalizations**. The danger of allness statements is that you may begin to believe them and to **prejudge** other people unfairly based on them. Therefore, be careful not to overgeneralize; remember that each individual is unique.

Fact-inference confusion occurs when people respond to something as if they have actually observed it when, in reality, they have merely drawn a conclusion. While statements of fact can be made only after direct observation, **inferences** can be made before, during, or after an occurrence. No observation is necessary. The key distinction is that in statements of inference people can **speculate** about and interpret what they *think* occurred. Like bypassing and allness statements, fact-inference confusion can lead to **inaccuracy** and misunderstanding.

—Adapted from Beebe and Masterson, *Communication in Small Groups*, Sixth Edition, pp. 120–122.

1. symbolically: using symbols

2. capacity: capability, mental ability

3. empower: give power to

4. impede: hinder, obstruct

5. compounded: increased, added to

6. generalizations: general conclusions based on particular instances

7. prejudge: judge beforehand

8. inferences: conclusions derived from knowledge or evidence

9. speculate: meditate on, reflect, conjecture

10. inaccuracy: mistakes, error

Read the following passage and use your knowledge of word parts and context to figure out the meaning of each boldfaced word or phrase. Write a synonym or definition in the space provided. Consult a dictionary if necessary.

Built into the retina of the human eye are about 130 million **photoreceptor** cells called rods and cones because of their shapes. Cones are **stimulated** by bright light and can distinguish color, but they do not function in night vision. Rods are extremely sensitive to light and enable us to see in dim light at night, though only in shades of gray. Rods are found in the greatest **density** at the outer edges of the retina, and are completely absent from the fovea, the retina's center of focus.

How do rods and cones detect light? Each rod and cone contains an array of **membranous** discs containing light-absorbing visual pigments. Rods contain a visual pigment called rhodopsin, which functions by absorbing dim light. Cones contain visual pigments called **photopsins**, which absorb bright, colored light. We have three types of cones, each containing a different type of photopsin. All three types of cones absorb a wide range of colors, and together they can detect virtually any color in the visible **spectrum** (between ultraviolet and infrared). Color blindness results from a **deficiency** in one or more types of cones.

Like all **receptor** cells, rods and cones are stimulus transducers. When rhodopsin and photopsin absorb light, they change chemically, and the change alters the **permeability** of the cell's membrane. The resulting receptor potentials trigger a complex **integration** process that actually begins in the retina.

—Adapted from Campbell, Mitchell, and Reece,
Biology: Concepts and Connections, Third Edition, p. 593.
Copyright © 2000. Reprinted by permission
of Pearson Education, Inc.

1. photoreceptor: <u>receiving light</u>

2. stimulated: <u>made active</u>

3. density: <u>compactness</u>

4. membranous: <u>consisting of a thin, pliable layer</u>

5. photopsins: <u>pigments that absorb light</u>

6. spectrum: <u>series or range of color</u>

7. deficiency: <u>a lack or shortage</u>

8. receptor: <u>cell that receives and responds to stimuli</u>

9. permeability: <u>ability to pass through or penetrate</u>

10. integration: <u>joining or uniting, bringing parts together</u>

LEARN MORE ABOUT WORD PARTS by visiting the following Web site:

Practice Quizzes with Greek and Latin Roots
    http://english.glendale.cc.ca.us/roots.html

PART FOUR

Vocabulary for the Twenty-First Century

SECTION A | Words on Loan: Foreign Words and Phrases

Umbrella, Iowa, tornado, pretzel, banjo, and *stove*—all of these are words that English speakers know and use. But did you know that *umbrella* was originally an Italian word (ombrella)? The word *Iowa* is an American Indian word that originally meant "drowsy ones." *Tornado* is a Spanish word; *pretzel* is a German word; *banjo* is an African word; and *stove* is a Dutch word. Each of these words has become an ordinary English word, but each was originally borrowed from another language.

Over hundreds of years, thousands of words have been borrowed from other languages in this manner, gradually becoming part of our standard English vocabulary. Often a change in spelling or pronunciation occurred as each word was adopted.

There are a few words and phrases, however, that are taken directly from a foreign language and retain their original pronunciation and spelling. Often, there is not a word or phrase in English that carries exactly the same meaning or expresses it in such a concise manner. An example is the French phrase *faux pas.* Its direct translation is "false step." It has come to mean a social blunder—an embarrassing, unintentional social error. If, for example, in a conversation with a sightless person, you said, "Don't you see?" meaning don't you understand, you might feel as if you made a *faux pas.* Your question was not quite the right thing to ask and you felt embarrassed. There is no single word or phrase that expresses exactly this situation in English, so the French phrase is used. This section presents a list of common foreign words and phrases that are frequently used by English speakers and writers.

Since the largest number of words and phrases have been borrowed from Latin and French, lists of common Latin and French words and phrases follow.

Useful Latin Words and Phrases

ad nauseam (ăd nô′zē-əm) Adverb. To a disgusting or ridiculous degree, causing disgust or boredom, to the point of nausea. The speaker repeated his sales pitch *ad nauseam.*

bona fide (bō′nə fīd′) Adjective. In good faith, sincere, authentic, genuine. The real estate agent thought the purchase offer was *bona fide.*

caveat emptor (kä′vē-ät ĕmp′tôr′) Noun. Let the buyer beware. The buyer is responsible for making sound buying decisions. The consumer advocate urged his radio listeners to repeat the phrase *caveat emptor* whenever they shopped for a used car.

de facto (dā făk′tō) Adjective. Actual. What is done, whether lawful or not. *De facto* racial segregation still exists in some parts of the country.

et cetera (ĕt sĕt′ər-ə) Noun. Abbreviated *etc.* And so forth, and so on. A number of unspecified similar items. On our trip to the Southwest we visited historical sites, national parks, *etc.*

modus operandi (mō′dəs ŏp′ə-răn′dē) Noun. A method, style, or manner of working or functioning. Beginning each class with a review of the prior lecture followed by a brief anecdote was Professor Yu's *modus operandi*.

non sequitur (nŏn sĕk′wĭ-tər) Noun. A statement or conclusion that does not follow from the evidence that preceded it. My neighbor made a *non sequitur* when he said, "It's raining because I washed my car this morning."

per annum (pər ăn′əm) Adverb. Annually or by the year. The library's subscription to the periodical is renewed *per annum*.

per capita (pər kăp′ĭ-tə) Adverb. Per person or by a fixed unit or group of population. Among nonwhite households, the average cost of transportation is $1212 *per capita*.

per diem (pər dē′əm) Adverb. By the day, per day. The laborers were paid $50 *per diem*.

persona non grata (pər-sō′nə nŏn grä′tə) Adjective. A person who is unacceptable or unwelcome. Often used as reference to a foreign government policy or decision. The former congressman was a *persona non grata* in Argentina.

postmortem (pōst-môr′təm) Adjective. After death or following a difficult or unpleasant event. A *postmortem* examination revealed the victim died of head wounds. At a *postmortem* conference, the sales staff analyzed their failure to win the multimillion-dollar contract.

status quo (stā′təs kwō) Noun. The way things are, an existing state of affairs. The presidential candidate promised to maintain the *status quo* of the social security system.

vice versa (vī′sə vûr′sə) Adverb. The other way around, with the order reversed. James suspected Martha and *vice versa*.

EXERCISE 4-1

Match the Latin word or phrase in column A with its meaning in column B. Write your answer in the space provided.

	Column A	Column B
1. _g_	non sequitur	a. By the day, per day
2. _i_	et cetera	b. A person who is unacceptable or unwelcome
3. _a_	per diem	c. The way things are, an existing state of affairs
4. _h_	modus operandi	d. Per person or by a fixed unit or group of population
5. _e_	per annum	e. Annually or by the year
6. _f_	caveat emptor	f. Let the buyer beware, the buyer is responsible for making sound buying decisions
7. _c_	status quo	g. A statement or conclusion that does not follow from the evidence that preceded it
8. _d_	per capita	h. A method, style, or manner of working or functioning
9. _j_	de facto	i. And so forth, and so on
10. _b_	persona non grata	j. What is done, whether lawful or not

Using the list of Latin words and phrases above, supply a word or phrase that fits the meaning of each of the following sentences.

EXAMPLE: The catalog contained dolls, trucks, electronic games, _____etc._____

1. He has been ____persona non grata____ at the restaurant ever since he insulted the chef.

2. The couple went on and on _____ad nauseam_____ about their trip to the Everglades.

3. All of my expenses at the convention were paid, in addition to a $100 _____per diem_____.

4. The sign over the flea market entrance warned shoppers with the words:
    ____Caveat Emptor____!

5. The pickpocket's ____modus operandi____ was to create a distraction by dropping a large package in a crowd.

6. We shook hands and parted, satisfied that we had made a _____bona fide_____ agreement.

7. The board of directors wanted to shake up the _____status quo_____ by hiring a female president.

8. After every loss, the coach conducted a _____postmortem_____ in which he discussed what went wrong during the game.

9. Li thought her sister was being difficult, and _____vice versa_____.

10. "The doorbell rang because I had just gotten in the bathtub" is a _____non sequitur_____. ■

Useful French Words and Phrases

avant-garde (ä′vänt-gärd′) Noun. People active in the invention of new ideas or techniques in a particular field. The Computer Task Group was considered *avant-garde.* Adjective. Describing an innovative or creative person or group. Jackson Pollack was considered an *avant-garde* artist.

carte blanche (kärt blänsh′) Noun. Freedom to use one's own judgment or authority, unconditional authority to act. In negotiating the new contract, the sales director was given *carte blanche.*

cause célèbre (kōz′ sä-lĕb′rə) Noun. A situation or issue involving widespread interest, public concern, or debate. The young illegal immigrant became a *cause celebre* last year.

coup (ko͞o) Noun. A sudden clever move or action. Persuading several Republicans to vote against the bill was quite a *coup* for the governor.

double entendre (dŭb′əl ä-tän′drə). Noun. A word or expression with two meanings; one of the meanings is often improper or indelicate. The comedy act contained so many *double entendres* that we understood why children were not admitted.

esprit de corps (ĕ-sprē′ də kôr′) Noun. Group spirit, comradeship. The sales team needs *esprit de corps* to work well together.

fait accompli (fā′tä-kôn-plē′) Noun. An accomplished fact, an irreversible or unchangeable act or decision. The family move to Arizona is a *fait accompli.*

faux pas (fō′ pä′) Noun. An embarrassing social blunder. The attorney's *faux pas* made the jury laugh aloud.

joie de vivre (zhwä′ də vē′vrə) Noun. Joy of living, enjoyment of life. Martin's *joie de vivre* is evident through his carefree lifestyle.

laissez-faire (lĕs′ā fâr′). Noun. The principle that business should operate without government interference and regulation; the principle of allowing others to do as they please. Nick had a *laissez-faire* attitude about the tenants in his building.

nouveau riche (nōō′vō rēsh′). Noun. A person who has recently become rich, especially in a showy manner. Computer gurus who have started dot-com companies are among the *nouveau riche*.

savoir faire (săv′wär-fār′) Noun. Knowledge of the right thing to do or say, social grace or tact. Cary Grant was an actor who always projected a certain *savoir faire*, both on screen and off.

tête-à-tête (tāt ′ə tāt′) Adverb or adjective. Two together in private. Noun. A private conversation between two people. The two friends were engaged in a *tête-à-tête*.

vis-à-vis (vē′z-ə-vē′). Preposition. Face to face with, compared with. The earnings report was a disappointment *vis-à-vis* the optimism earlier in the year.

EXERCISE 4-3

Match the French word or phrase in column A with its meaning in column B. Write the letter of your answer in the space provided.

	Column A		Column B
1. __k__	avant-garde	a.	Freedom to use one's own judgment or authority, unconditional authority to act
2. __g__	esprit de corps	b.	A situation or issue involving widespread interest, public concern, or debate
3. __i__	tête-à-tête	c.	A sudden clever move or action
4. __a__	carte blanche	d.	An accomplished fact, an irreversible or unchangeable act or decision
5. __l__	joie de vivre	e.	The principle that business should operate without government interference and regulation; the principle of allowing others to do as they please
6. __j__	savoir faire	f.	A word or expression with two meanings; one of the meanings is often improper or indelicate
7. __f__	double entendre	g.	Group spirit, comradeship
8. __b__	cause célèbre	h.	Face to face with, compared with
9. __d__	fait accompli	i.	Two together in private; a private conversation between two people
10. __e__	coup	j.	Knowledge of the right thing to do or say; social grace or tact
11. __h__	vis-à-vis	k.	People active in the invention of new ideas or techniques in a particular field
12. __c__	laissez-faire	l.	Joy of living, enjoyment of life

Using the list of French words and phrases above, supply a word or phrase that fits the meaning of each of the following sentences.

1. She considered it a _____coup_____ to host the national convention in her hometown.

2. A certain _____esprit de corps_____ developed among the people who had been stranded at the airport.

3. We were given _____carte blanche_____ with regard to ordering supplies for the festival.

4. The many _____double entendres_____ in the film made me wish I had taken my mother to another movie.

5. During our brief and hectic visit, we were able to find time for a quiet_____tête-à-tête_____.

6. The decision to accept the job offer was a _____fait accompli_____.

7. Wyclef Jean is too _____avant-garde_____ a musician to appeal to the masses.

8. The south side of town was mainly "old money," but the west side was strictly for the _____nouveau riche_____.

9. We realized our _____faux pas_____ when he introduced the young lady as his wife, not his daughter.

10. The new chairperson's hands-on approach to running the business was a departure from her predecessor's _____laissez-faire_____ style.

| SECTION B | **Words Have Feelings, Too: Connotative Meanings** |

If you were wearing a leather-looking jacket that was made out of manmade fibers, would you prefer that it be called *fake* or *synthetic*?

Would you rather be part of a *crowd* or *mob*?

Would you rather be called a *college student* or a *college kid*?

Each of the above pairs of words has basically the same meaning. A *crowd* and a *mob* are both groups of people. Both *college student* and *college kid* refer to someone who attends college. If the words have similar meanings, why did you choose *crowd* rather than *mob* and *college student* rather than *college kid*? While the pairs of words have similar primary meanings, they carry different shades of meaning; each creates a different image or association in your mind. This section will explore these shades of meaning, called connotative meanings.

All words have one or more standard meanings. These meanings are called *denotative meanings.* Think of them as those meanings listed in the dictionary. They tell us what the word names. Many words also have connotative meanings. *Connotative meanings* include the feelings and associations that may accompany a word. For example, the denotative meaning of *mother* is female parent. However, the word carries many connotations. For many, *mother* suggests a warm, loving, caring person. Let's take another example, the word *home*. Its denotative meaning is "a place where one lives," but to many its connotative meaning suggests comfort, privacy, and coziness. Figure 4.1 shows some connotative meanings of the word "mother."

Writers and speakers use connotative meanings to stir emotions or to bring to mind positive or negative associations. Suppose a writer is describing how someone walks. The writer could choose words such as *strut, stroll, swagger,* or *amble.* Do you see how each creates a different image of the person? Connotative meanings, then, are powerful tools of language. When you read, be alert for meanings suggested by the author's word choice. When writing or speaking, be sure to choose words with appropriate connotations.

Connotations can vary from individual to individual. The denotative meaning for the word *flag* is a piece of cloth used as a national emblem. To many, the American flag is a symbol of patriotism and love of one's country. To some people, though, it may mean an interesting decoration to place on their clothing. The word *cat* to cat lovers suggests a fluffy, furry, cuddly animal. To those who are allergic to cats, however, the word *cat* connotes discomfort and avoidance—itchy eyes, a runny nose, etc.

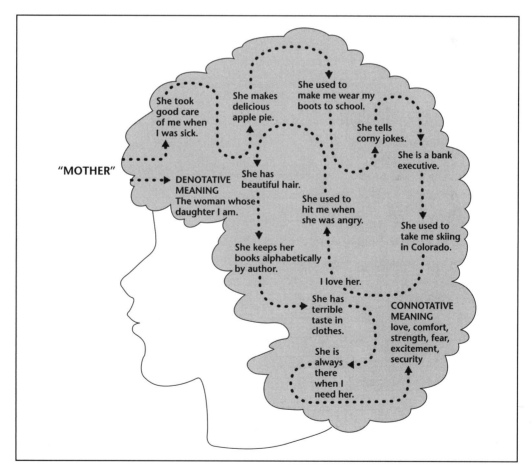

FIGURE 4–1 One person's connotations for the word "mother."

EXERCISE 4-5

Discuss the differences in connotative meaning of each of the following pairs or sets of words. Consult a dictionary, if necessary. Answers will vary.

EXAMPLE: To improve: **mend—reform**

Mend implies repairing something that is broken; reform means changing something,

often a document or law, to improve it or eliminate its faults.

1. To find fault: **admonish—reprimand**

Admonish implies giving advice or warning so that a fault can be rectified or a danger avoided

(more positive), whereas reprimand refers to sharp, often angry, criticism (more negative).

2. A competitor: **rival—opponent**

A rival is one who seeks to equal or surpass another, and an opponent is one who opposes,

resists, or combats opposition.

3. Working together: **accomplice—colleague**

An accomplice is one who aids a lawbreaker in a criminal activity (negative), whereas a colleague

is an associate, a peer, a fellow member of a profession (positive).

4. Stated briefly: **pithy—concise**

Pithy is forceful and brief, precisely meaningful (more negative); concise is clear and succinct,

expressing much in few words (more positive).

5. Long lasting: **perpetual—interminable—eternal**

Perpetual means lasting for eternity or continuing indefinitely (as in perpetual friendship);

interminable is more negative, as something endless, tiresomely long, wearisome (an

interminable wait); and eternal is without beginning or end, seemingly endless, with a spiritual

connotation.

6. Inactive: **idle—lethargic—languid**

Idle is not employed or busy, avoiding work (negative connotation of laziness); lethargic is a

sluggish, drowsy dullness possibly caused by illness, fatigue or overwork; and languid implies

a lack of energy or spirit in one who is satiated by a life of luxury or pleasure.

7. Ability: **proficiency—aptitude—dexterity**

Proficiency implies a learned competence; aptitude implies an inherent ability or talent; and

dexterity can mean skill or grace, especially in the use of hands, or mental skill and cleverness.

8. Old: **antique—old-fashioned—obsolete—dated**

Antique is typical of an earlier period, belonging to ancient times (implies value); old-fashioned

is of a style or method formerly in vogue, now outdated; obsolete is no longer in use, outmoded in

design, style or construction; and dated is old-fashioned

9. Cautious: **wary—vigilant—careful**

   Wary is on guard, watchful, characterized by caution; vigilant is also watchful, alert, aware (may

   imply more aggressive watchfulness); and careful is attentive to potential danger, error, or harm.

10. Trip: **excursion—pilgrimage—vacation—tour**

    An excursion is a pleasure trip or outing; pilgrimage implies a spiritual aspect, as in a journey to

    a sacred place; vacation is a holiday from work; and tour is a trip to various places for business,

    pleasure, or instruction.

EXERCISE 4-6

For each of the following sentences, underline the word in parentheses that best completes the sentence. Consult a dictionary, if necessary.

1. The price of the dinner was (<u>exorbitant</u>, extravagant).

2. The discipline policy at the boarding school was (stiff, <u>rigid</u>).

3. Using coupons at the grocery store is one way of being (<u>frugal</u>, stingy).

4. Jay had several friends with tattoos, but he never felt (influenced, <u>pressured</u>) to get one himself.

5. The neighbors were embroiled in a (<u>dispute</u>, debate) over property lines.

6. The restaurant manager (<u>warned</u>, threatened) us that it could be well over an hour before we were seated.

7. The couple (hesitated, <u>wavered</u>) several times before finally deciding to put their house on the market.

8. The millionaire made his fortune through several (<u>bold</u>, brash) investments.

9. He had a (forcible, <u>forceful</u>) personality that was difficult to ignore.

10. The physician is (<u>dedicated</u>, pledged) to the well-being of her patients.

SECTION C Not Saying What You Mean: Euphemisms

My aunt passed away.

Where is the men's room?

I work for the sanitation department.

What do each of these sentences have in common? Each uses an expression called a euphemism—a word or phrase that is used in place of a word that is unpleasant, embarrassing, or otherwise objectionable. The expression *passed away* replaces the word *died*, *men's room* is a substitute for *toilet*, and *sanitation* is a more pleasing term than *garbage*.

The word *euphemism* comes from the Greek roots *eu-*, meaning "sounding good," and *-pheme*, meaning "speech." Euphemisms have a long history going back to ancient languages and cultures. Ancient people thought of names as extensions of the things themselves. To know and say the name of a person or object gave the speaker power over that person or object. Thus, calling something by its name was avoided, even forbidden. God, Satan, deceased relatives, and hunted animals would often be referred to indirectly. For example, in one culture God was called the Kindly One; the bear was called the Grandfather. Today, many euphemisms are widely used in both spoken and written language. Here are a few more examples:

The objective of the air strike was to <u>neutralize the enemy</u>. (kill the enemy)

Some <u>collateral damage</u> occurred as a result of the air strike. (death to civilians)

When it is hot, people <u>perspire</u>. (sweat)

Euphemisms tend to minimize or downplay the importance or seriousness of something. They are often used in politics and advertising. They can be used to camouflage actions or events that may be unacceptable to readers or listeners if bluntly explained. For example, the word *casualties of war* may be used instead of the phrase *dead soldiers* to lessen the impact of the attack. To say that a politician's statement was *at variance with the truth* is less forceful than to say that the politician *lied*.

When you speak or write, be sure to avoid euphemisms that obscure or interfere with your intended meaning. Euphemisms can lead your listeners or readers to believe that you have something to hide or that you are not being completely truthful with them.

EXERCISE 4-7

For each of the boldfaced euphemisms, write a substitution that does not minimize or avoid the basic meaning of the term.

EXAMPLE: The theater had only one **ladies room**. _____toilet for women_____

1. The search continued for the **remains** of the victims of the air crash. _____bodies_____

2. The advertising campaign was an **incomplete success**. _____failure_____

3. The presidential aide was accused of spreading **disinformation**.
   _____deliberately misleading information (lies)_____

4. We took our broken refrigerator to the **sanitary landfill**. _____garbage dump_____

5. The company announced that it would be **downsizing** several hundred employees over the next few months. _____firing_____

6. The business recorded a **negative cash flow** last month. _____loss of money_____

7. We noticed that she **was carrying a little extra weight**. _____overweight, heavy_____

8. The car dealership sold both new and **previously owned** automobiles.
   _____used_____

9. Witnesses reported that the two men **exchanged words** before the gun was fired.
   _____argued_____

10. The veterinarian recommended that the elderly cat be **put to sleep**. _____killed_____

SECTION D | Untangling a Tangle of Words: Doublespeak

The letter from the Air Force colonel in charge of safety said that rocket boosters weighing more than 300,000 pounds "have an explosive force upon surface impact that is sufficient to exceed the accepted overpressure threshold of physiological damage for the exposed personnel."[1]

What does the colonel's statement mean in simple words? *Answer:* If a 300,000 pound rocket falls on a person, it will kill him or her.

The language the colonel used is an example of doublespeak. Here are a few more examples. Can you translate each of the following phrases into simple language?

1. chronically experienced citizens _____

2. ground-mounted confirmatory route markers _____

3. vertically deployed antipersonnel devices _____

The answers are (1) senior citizens, (2) road signs, (3) bombs.

Doublespeak is deliberately unclear or evasive language. Often, it exaggerates or overstates information that could be expressed simply. William Lutz, an expert on doublespeak, defines it as "language that pretends to communicate but does not."[2]

Doublespeak uses euphemisms (see Section C), but it tangles language in other ways, as well, that are intended to confuse or overwhelm the listener or reader. Doublespeak may also use (1) technical language that is likely to be unfamiliar to the audience, (2) inflated language, or words that tend to make something seem more important or complex than it really is, and (3) long, polysyllabic words. It may scramble the order of words in a sentence to create confusion or avoid giving complete information. For example, the passive voice may be used to avoid saying who performed an action. In the sentence "The bombs were released, injuring many civilians," we do not know who released the bombs.

In your own writing, avoid doublespeak at all costs; it is the opposite of clear, concise expression. When reading doublespeak, be suspicious of the writer's motives. Ask yourself: Why is the writer being purposefully evasive or unclear? What is he or she trying to hide?

EXERCISE 4-8

Untangle each of the following examples of doublespeak and write a translation in simple English.
Answers will vary.

EXAMPLE: Most hospitals are reluctant to publicize negative patient care outcomes.

Hospitals are reluctant to publicize patient deaths.

1. Human rights violations in Country X included the "unlawful or arbitrary deprivation of human life." (U.S. State Department)

People in Country X were killed.

2. Corporations involved in staff reduction activities often offer excessed employees reemployment engineering.

Corporations often help the employees they have fired find other jobs.

3. Preliminary reports showed a negative gain in test scores in the state's public schools.

Test scores for public school students in this state went down.

4. Please allow the more vertically challenged individuals to come to the front of the group so they may have a clearer line of sight.

Let the shorter people move to the front so they can see better.

5. The merchandise order you have placed cannot be accommodated due to current shortages in inventory.

We are out of the item you want to buy.

6. Your request for assistance will be processed in a timely manner by customer service representatives in the order in which it was received.

You must wait until we get to your call.

7. A corporate climate specialist will join us today to facilitate the positive exchange of ideas.

This person who specializes in employee relations will run the meeting.

8. After the less-than-positive earnings of last quarter, it has become necessary to eliminate redundancies in various areas of the company.

Last quarter's earnings were poor so we have to fire some people.

9. The couple entered interrelational therapy in an effort to work out some of their compatibility issues.

They went to a marriage counselor because they weren't getting along.

10. A low pressure system will be moving into the area later this evening, bringing with it the possibility of an accumulation of precipitation.

Looks like rain!

LEARN MORE ABOUT DOUBLESPEAK by visiting the following Web sites:

http://www.lssu.edu/banished/current/default.html
http://www.cord.edu/faculty/sprunger/e315/dbltk.html

Where Do New Words Come From?

Here are a few newly coined (created) words. Do you know their meanings?

- slamming

- senior moment

- sky surfing

- zettabyte

Answers: Slamming is the change of long-distance telephone service without the customer's permission. A *senior moment* is a brief lapse of memory or confusion. *Sky surfing* is aerial skateboarding. A *zettabyte* is a measure of a computer's memory capacity; it is one sextillion bytes.

New words enter our language each year. These new words are called *neologisms.*

English is a language that is constantly changing; new words are added and words that have become outdated are classified as obsolete. One way new words enter our language is through social and cultural change. Many of our great grandparents never heard of words like *taco, quiche, croissant, piña colada, tofu,* and *pita bread*—nor ventured to taste the foods they described. Now these words and food items have become standard fare.

Computer technology has brought hundreds of new words into our language. Our grandparents never heard of *e-mail, CD-ROMs, modems,* and so forth. Here are a few other ways new words enter our language:

- People make up new words. Writers and speakers create new words. It is estimated that one-tenth of the words Shakespeare used were never used before. Developers of new products make up words to describe their products. The word *sneaker* entered our language this way.

- Words are created by error. According to the *Oxford English Dictionary,* at least 350 English words came into existence because of typographical errors or misreadings. Others came into existence by mishearings (people think they hear a word pronounced a certain way and pronounce it that way themselves). Because of such errors, for example, *shamefast* became *shamefaced.*

- Meanings of existing words change. Often a word itself does not change. Rather its meaning does. For example, *tell* used to mean *count.* (Think of a *bank teller.*)

- Words are shortened:

  Examination has become *exam.*

  Gymnasium has become *gym.*

  Laboratory has become *lab.*

- Words are combined to make new words. (Some are compound words; others may be two separate words; others are hyphenated.)

  Seaplane

  High school

  Half-moon

EXERCISE 4-9

Each of the following words recently entered the English language and appeared in one of the more recently revised dictionaries. Write the meaning of each, consulting a recent hardcopy dictionary or using an online dictionary.

EXAMPLE: cross trainer: <u>A type of athletic shoe designed for use with a variety of sports.</u>

1. carjacking: <u>an incident in which a usually armed individual forces the driver of a car to give up the vehicle or drive it and the assailant to a specified location</u>

2. antiglare: <u>treatment on computer screens that reduces reflected glare by absorbing or diffusing light</u>

3. energy bar: <u>high-calorie food item promoted as an energy source for hikers, campers, athletes, etc.</u>

4. megaplex: <u>movie theater with multiple screens</u>

5. e-tailing: <u>retailing done on the Internet (electronically)</u>

6. Gen Y'ers: <u>category of people in the generation born after baby boomers and generation X (post-1980)</u>

7. date rape: <u>an incidence of forced sexual intercourse by one of two individuals who are dating</u>

8. fashionista: <u>slightly sarcastic reference to a person who is a fashion enthusiast</u>

9. spamming: <u>sending unsolicited, usually commercial, e-mail to a large number of recipients</u>

10. televangelist: <u>an evangelist (preacher) who conducts religious services on television</u>

Each of the following is a newly created word or phrase listed on a Web site that features neologisms. Try to figure out the meaning of each. *Note:* Most of them are not yet accepted as authentic English words; if they do not appear in the dictionary, they should not be used in academic writing.

EXAMPLE: body Nazis: workout fanatics who look down on anyone who does not work out

1. baggravation (*Hint:* think about airlines and baggage problems):
   a feeling of annoyance and anger when everyone's baggage but your own has arrived on the baggage carousel at the airport

2. mouse potato (*Hint:* think computers and couch potato):
   one who spends an excessive amount of time in front of the computer screen

3. blamestorming (*Hint:* modify brainstorming):
   sitting around in a group discussing whose fault it is that a project failed or a deadline was missed

4. forklift upgrade: describes the remedy when an entire system needs to be replaced, rather than one component or part (as in "That PC needs a forklift upgrade.")

5. Gutenberg: a person who prints off all of his or her e-mails and other electronic data; reference to Johann Gutenberg, the German printer who invented movable type (as in "No wonder he runs out of paper all the time, he's such a Gutenberg.")

6. netizen: a person who spends an excessive amount of time on the Internet (Internet + citizen)

7. mallrats: preteens and teenagers who spend an excessive amount of time socializing at a shopping mall

8. flaming: writing angry e-mail messages

9. netiquette: rules of etiquette for online interactions; e.g., typing a message in all uppercase letters is the same as shouting

10. losingest: in last place, worst off, behind all the rest; e.g., "The Decatur Bladers had the losingest record in the over-30 softball league."

LEARN MORE ABOUT NEOLOGISMS by visiting the following Web site:

http://www.owlnet.rice.edu/~ling215/NewWords

SECTION F Let Your Creativity Show: Using Figurative Language

The cake tasted like sawdust.

Her answer was as unexpected as a white tiger appearing in my yard.

Today, my boss, Martha Yarfield, is as nervous as an expectant father.

You know that a cake cannot really be made of sawdust, that answers are not white tigers, and that the boss is not an expectant father. Instead, you know that the writer means that the cake was dry and tasteless, that the answer was totally unexpected, and that the boss is full of anxious anticipation.

Each of these statements is an example of *figurative language*—a way of describing something that makes sense on an imaginative or creative level, but not on a factual or literal level. None of the above statements is literally true, but each is meaningful. In many figurative expressions, one thing is compared with another for some quality they have in common. Two unlike objects, the cake and sawdust, share the characteristic of dryness.

The purpose of figurative language is to paint a word picture that will help the reader or listener visualize how something looks, feels, or smells. Figurative language allows the writer or speaker the opportunity to be creative and to express attitudes and opinions without directly stating them. Figurative language is used widely in literature, as well as many forms of expressive writing. Here are a few examples:

- I will speak daggers to her, but use none. (Shakespeare, *Hamlet*)
- An aged man is but a paltry thing, / a tattered coat upon a stick . . . (W. B. Yeats, *Sailing to Byzantium*)
- Time is but the stream I go a-fishing in. (Henry David Thoreau, *Walden*)
- Announced by all the trumpets of the sky, / arrives the snow . . . (Ralph Waldo Emerson, *The Snowstorm*)

The two most common types of figurative language are metaphors and similes. A *simile* uses the word *like* or *as* to make a comparison. A *metaphor* states or implies that one thing *is* another thing. If you say, "Mary's dress looks <u>like</u> a whirlwind of color," you have created a simile. If you say, "Mary's dress <u>is</u> a whirlwind of color," you have created a metaphor. Notice that each compares two unlike things, the dress and the whirlwind.

EXERCISE 4-11

For each of the figurative expressions indicated in each sentence, circle the choice that best explains its meaning.

1. It was **an uphill battle** to get the insurance claim approved.

   a. dangerous

   b. extremely difficult

   c. physically tiring

   d. complicated

2. His face **clouded over** as soon as she said no.
   a. looked unhappy
   b. cleared up
   c. cooled off
   d. was shaded

3. She asked for the favor in a voice **dripping with honey.**
   a. sentimental
   b. overly sweet
   c. unpleasant
   d. sticky

4. At sunset, the surface of the lake was **like a piece of glass.**
   a. sharp
   b. smooth
   c. wavy
   d. hard

5. After dining at the all-you-can-eat buffet, he was **as full as a tick.**
   a. still hungry
   b. like a parasite
   c. rude
   d. stuffed with food

6. She politely asked her visitors to leave, but **icicles were hanging on every word.**
   a. it was winter
   b. she had a sparkling voice
   c. she spoke in a cold, unwelcoming manner
   d. she used fancy words

7. As he dozed in the hammock, the sun slowly moved across the yard and dropped **a soft, golden blanket** on him.
   a. warmth
   b. yellow leaves
   c. rain
   d. pollen

8. The sound of the chainsaw outside her window was **like a dentist drilling on her nerves.**
   a. a pleasant humming
   b. a sound she could ignore
   c. an extremely unpleasant sound
   d. an important and necessary sound

9. His birthday money was **burning a hole in his pocket!**
   a. on fire
   b. too heavy for his pocket to hold
   c. causing people to look at him
   d. making him anxious to spend it

10. Our computer is **a dinosaur.**
    a. huge
    b. awkward
    c. heavy
    d. outdated

LEARN MORE ABOUT FIGURATIVE LANGUAGE by visiting the following Web site:

http://www.westga.edu/~scarter/Figurative_Language1.htm

Stretching Your Thinking with Words: Analogies

Can you fill in the blank?

Up is to down as right is to _____ .

If you answered "left," you are correct. You have just completed an analogy. You can think of an analogy as a comparison made between sets of words. Understanding and working with analogies is an excellent means of sharpening your vocabulary as well. Analogies force you to use language, stretch your thinking, and strengthen your logical reasoning skills. Analogies also crop up on all sorts of standardized tests, so it is useful to be familiar with how they work. For example, various graduate school admission tests, licensing exams, civil service exams, and employment tests contain analogies.

An analogy is an abbreviated statement expressing the same relationship between two pairs of items. Analogies are usually written in the following format:

black : white :: dark : light

This can be read in either of two ways:

1. *Black is to white as dark is to light.* (The words in each pair are opposites.)

2. *White has the same relationship to black as light does to dark.* (White is the opposite of black, and light is the opposite of dark.)

In analogies, the relationship between the words or phrases is critically important.

Analogies become problem-solving and critical-thinking exercises when one of the four items, usually the fourth, is left blank and you are instructed to supply or choose a correct answer.

Here are a few simple analogies that demonstrate how analogies work; supply a correct answer for each blank.

1. celery : vegetable :: orange : _____

2. shotgun : bullet :: bow : _____

3. video : watch :: audio : _____

4. hot : cold :: heavy : _____

5. hamburgers : Burger King :: chicken : _____

In the first analogy, the correct answer is fruit because celery is a type of vegetable and an orange is a type of fruit. Other answers should be (2) arrow, (3) listen, (4) light, and (5) KFC (or another fast-food restaurant featuring chicken).

Tips for Solving Analogies

The key to solving analogies is to analyze the relationship that exists between the first pair of words or between the first and third items. The relationship you uncover between the first pair must be expressed in the second pair.

Analogies typically explore several common relationships. These include:

1. Opposites—*Example:* yes : no :: stop : start

   (The words in each pair are opposites.)

2. Whole/part—*Example:* year : month :: week : day

   (A month is part of a year; a day is part of a week.)

3. Synonyms—*Example:* moist : damp :: happy : glad

   (The words in each pair are interchangeable.)

4. Categories—*Example:* dessert : cake :: meat : beef

   (Cake is a type of dessert; beef is a type of meat.)

5. Similarities—*Example:* lemon : orange :: celery : cabbage

   (The words in each pair are similar because they belong to the same category of things.)

6. Association or action—*Example:* train : conductor :: airplane : pilot

   (A conductor operates a train; a pilot operates a plane.)

In addition to the ability to analyze relationships, analogies often require background knowledge or information. For example, the following analogy requires that you know that red light waves are the longest while violet ones are the shortest.

red : longest :: violet :: (shortest)

EXERCISE 4-12

Complete each of the following sets of analogies by circling the appropriate word or phrase. Each set is increasingly more difficult. Check a dictionary for the meaning of unfamiliar terms.

Set I

1. sculptor : statue :: musician : _____
   - a. art
   - b. songwriters
   - c. music
   - d. notes

2. brush : painter :: pen : _____
   - a. pencil
   - b. book
   - c. paper
   - d. writer

3. coffee : cup :: hamburger : _____
   - a. beef
   - b. milkshake
   - c. bun
   - d. eat

4. halibut: fish :: lamb : _____
   - a. animal
   - b. chicken
   - c. mutton
   - d. wool

5. dress : wear :: apple : _____
   a. peel   c. fruit
   (b.) eat   d. food

6. tennis : ball :: hockey : _____
   a. stick   (c.) puck
   b. game   d. ice

7. like : dislike :: respect : _____
   a. inspect   c. admire
   b. expect   (d.) disrespect

8. snake : reptile :: whale : _____
   a. fish   c. ocean
   (b.) mammal   d. aquatic

9. word : sentence :: sentence : _____
   a. line   (c.) paragraph
   b. write   b. report

10. New Orleans : Louisiana :: Chicago : _____
    (a.) Illinois   c. Midwest
    b. Lake Michigan   d. Indiana

Set II

1. aviary : birds :: greenhouse : _____
   a. bugs   c. gardener
   (b.) plants   d. outdoors

2. Alps : Europe :: Rockies : _____
   (a.) North America   c. Switzerland
   b. mountains   d. Colorado

3. podiatrist : feet :: ophthalmologist : _____
   a. doctor   c. organs
   b. head   (d.) eyes

4. United States : president :: England : _____
   a. Great Britain   (c.) prime minister
   b. United Kingdom   d. monarchy

5. horn : honk :: whistle : _____
   a. shrill   c. lips
   (b.) blow   d. tune

6. Iowa : state :: Jupiter : _____

   (a.) planet

   b. space

   c. Mars

   d. moon

7. fresh : rancid :: unique : _____

   a. appearance

   b. characteristic

   c. rare

   (d.) common

8. Picasso : painter :: Shakespeare : _____

   a. plays

   (b.) writer

   c. literature

   d. words

9. hasten : speed up :: outdated : _____

   (a.) old-fashioned

   b. current

   c. slow

   d. timely

10. solar : sun :: lunar : _____

   a. planets

   b. earth

   (c.) moon

   d. stars

Set III

1. expunge : delete :: repel : _____

   (a.) resist

   b. erase

   c. remove

   d. attract

2. perceive : understand :: ostentatious : _____

   a. plain

   (b.) showy

   c. understated

   d. exterior

3. quart : pint :: 1 : _____

   a. 1

   (b.) 2

   c. 3

   d. 8

4. Allah : Islam :: God : _____

   a. America

   b. Jesus

   (c.) Christianity

   d. Creator

5. United States : dollar :: Japan : _____

   a. money

   b. dollar

   c. peso

   (d.) yen

6. odometer : mileage :: barometer : _____

   (a.) atmospheric pressure

   b. temperature

   c. weather

   d. precipitation

7. present : past :: sit : _____

   (a.) sat

   b. walk

   c. sitting

   d. stand

8. old age : geriatrics :: infancy : _____

    a. babies   c. childhood

    b. families   (d.) pediatrics

9. Adam Smith : capitalism :: Karl Marx : _____

    a. German   c. society

    (b.) communism   d. atheism

10. export : import :: malignant : _____

    a. cancerous   (c.) benign

    b. tumor   d. health

LEARN MORE ABOUT ANALOGIES by visiting the following Web site:

http://www.puzz.com

Try the analogies test.

SECTION H   Is It *Lie* or *Lay?* Commonly Confused Words

Which sentence in each of the following pairs is correct?

- *Lay* the package on the table.

  Lie the package on the table.

- The couple will divide the settlement *between* them.

  The couple will divide the settlement *among* them.

- The police were unable to *elicit* any information from the accomplice.

  The police were unable to *illicit* any information from the accomplice.

Answers: **The first sentence in each pair is correct.**

There are many word pairs or groups, such as those above, that are commonly confused and misused. Use the following list to be sure you use words correctly in your speech and writing.

Accept To receive. She will **accept** the gift.

Except Other than. Everyone was invited **except** me.

Adapt To adjust or accommodate. The children **adapted** easily to life in Panama.

Adopt To accept and put into effect. The council members agreed to **adopt** the new budget beginning in May.

Advice Guidance or information. My teacher offered **advice** on how to study.

Advise To offer guidance. My teacher **advised** me to drop the course.

Affect To influence. Smoking **affects** one's health.

Effect Result. The **effects** of smoking are obvious.

Allusion Indirect reference or hint. Her **allusions** about his weight were embarrassing.

Illusion False idea or appearance. Cosmetic surgery creates the **illusion** of youth.

Between Refers to two things or people. My wife and I will divide the household chores **between** us.

Among Refers to three or more people or things. The vote was evenly divided **among** the four candidates.

Beside Next to, along the side of. He wants to sit **beside** you.

Besides In addition to. **Besides** the regular players, the team has three reserve players.

Bring Describes movement of an object toward you. **Bring** me the newspaper.

Take Describes movement away from you. **Take** these letters to the mailbox.

Censor To edit or ban from the public. The school board will **censor** the controversial novel from the library.

Censure To criticize or condemn publicly. The mayor was **censured** for misusing public funds.

Cite To summon to appear in court; to quote. I couldn't believe I was **cited** for jaywalking. OR She **cited** Toni Morrison in her acceptance speech.

Sight Something seen. The best **sight** in the world is your own child's smile.

Site Location. The **site** for the new civic center has not yet been determined.

Complement To add to or go with. Their personalities **complement** one another.

Compliment To praise or flatter. I must **compliment** you on your quick wit.

Conscience Awareness of the moral right and wrong of your own actions. Her **conscience** has been bothering her ever since she told that lie.

Conscious Aware or alert. He remained **conscious** during the surgery.

Continual Repeated regularly. We have enjoyed everything about our house except for the **continual** need to pay the mortgage.

Continuous Happens without stopping. They sailed **continuously** for two months before they reached land.

Coarse Rough. Stone-ground grits have a pleasantly **coarse** texture.

Course Class or path. Many students considered the film **course** their favorite. The **course** was quite hilly but we enjoyed the exercise.

Elicit To draw out or extract. It is sometimes difficult to **elicit** information from a teenager.

Illicit Unlawful, illegal. The mobsters were charged with several **illicit** activities, including gambling and extortion.

Eminent Something evident or outstanding. The **eminent** Dr. Sullivan will be the keynote speaker at the conference.

Imminent Something about to happen. Everyone felt sure that an announcement was **imminent**.

Explicit Clearly expressed. I gave her **explicit** instructions about taking care of the cats while we were out of town.

Implicit Implied or complete. We had an **implicit** agreement not to mention her first marriage. I trust him **implicitly**.

Farther At or to a greater distance. We hiked much **farther** than we had intended.

Further To a greater extent, more; or help forward. After grounding him, we sent him to his room to **further** contemplate his bad behavior. Her support went a long way toward **furthering** our cause.

Fewer A smaller number of persons or things. Every year, there seem to be **fewer** television programs that I really enjoy.

Less A smaller amount or to a smaller extent. However, there does seem to be **less** violence during prime time.

Good Satisfactory, adequate (adjective). Milo felt **good** about his performance on the final exam.

Well Satisfactorily, fortunately (adverb). Most of the class did very **well** on the bonus question.

Imply To suggest or state indirectly. I didn't mean to **imply** that you were a thief.

Infer To guess or conclude. There were no signs of forced entry, so the detective **inferred** that the intruder had a key to the house.

Its Of or relating to it or itself (adjective). The old barn is in terrible shape—**its** roof is about to fall in.

It's Contraction of *it is*. I'm taking the car to be serviced tomorrow because **it's** making an odd noise.

Lay To set down. Please **lay** those drawings on the table.

Lie To be in a horizontal position. I would like to **lie** down for a minute.

Loose Not rigidly fastened. Part of the problem with your car is the **loose** fan belt.

Lose To misplace or miss. Orinthia put the key in her pocket so she wouldn't **lose** it.

Principal Most important; a sum of money. The **principal** reason I've called you here today is to discuss your finances; the **principal** you invested with us six months ago has doubled!

Principle A rule or code of conduct. He refused to compromise his **principles** so he was fired.

Proceed To move forward. After obtaining a loan, we were able to **proceed** with our remodeling plans.

Precede To go before. The couple who **preceded** us in line bought the last pair of tickets.

Raise Collect or lift up. The booster club was able to **raise** $4,000 for the school's athletic teams. OR It was impossible to **raise** the windows because they had been painted shut.

Rise To get up or to move upward. We watched the hot-air balloons **rise** into the sky.

Set To place. Please **set** that vase down very carefully.

Sit To occupy a seat. Please **sit** wherever you'd like.

Stationary Fixed or unchanging. We bought a **stationary** bicycle so we could exercise during the winter.

Stationery Writing paper. She ordered new **stationery** with her initials embossed on it.

Than In comparison with. I like classical music better **than** rap.

Then At that time, next. First we went out to eat, **then** we decided to see a movie.

Their Of or relating to them or themselves. It's not **their** fault that they ran out of gas; **their** gas gauge was broken.

There Used to introduce a sentence (pronoun), or that place (noun). **There** is no time for dawdling; we'll have to hurry if we want to get **there** on time!

They're Contraction of *they are*. They promised to be on time, but **they're** always late.

Threw Past tense of to throw. The pitcher **threw** the ball as hard as he could.

Through From one side to the other, or finished. We decided to go **through** the forest instead of around it. OR After he injured his knee, he knew he was **through** with soccer.

To Toward (preposition); also used for marking a verb that follows as an infinitive (as in *to see*). They went **to** New England in October **to** see the fall colors.

Too Also, or very. We would have gone **too**, but the trip was **too** long.

Two A whole number meaning one more than one. The **two** men agreed to meet for coffee at **two** o'clock.

Weather Atmospheric conditions. The **weather** was stormy the whole time we were at the beach.

Whether If, in case, if it happens that. I plan to go, **whether** you join me or not.

Who's Contraction of *who is*. **Who's** going on the canoe trip?

Whose Of or relating to whom, especially as possessor. I wonder **whose** truck is parked in front of her house.

EXERCISE 4-13

Underline the correct word in parentheses to complete each of the following sentences.

1. Please (sit, <u>set</u>) my laptop on my desk (<u>beside</u>, besides) those papers.

2. It is my pleasure to (<u>accept</u>, except) your offer.

3. They had hoped to meet us for dinner before the play, but (<u>their</u>, they're, there) babysitter was late, so (their, <u>they're</u>, there) going to meet us (their, they're, <u>there</u>).

4. Baked apples make a delicious (<u>complement</u>, compliment) to roast pork.

5. My husband is (to, too, <u>two</u>) years younger (<u>than</u>, then) his brother.

6. We allowed the funeral procession to (<u>precede</u>, proceed) us, then we (preceded, <u>proceeded</u>) on our way.

7. The severe (<u>weather</u>, whether) had such an (affect, <u>effect</u>) on her that she gave (<u>explicit</u>, implicit) instructions not to be disturbed for the rest of the day.

8. A debate appeared to be (eminent, <u>imminent</u>), but I still had not decided (who's, <u>whose</u>) side I was on.

9. She made several (<u>allusions</u>, illusions) to his mysterious past, but we were unable to (imply, <u>infer</u>) what she was trying to (<u>imply</u>, infer).

10. Even though (its, <u>it's</u>) getting late, I'd like to drive you by the building (cite, sight, <u>site</u>).

LEARN MORE ABOUT VOCABULARY FOR THE TWENTY-FIRST CENTURY
by visiting the following Web sites:

1. Doublespeak Proverbs
   http://www.cord.edu/faculty/sprunger/e315/dbltk.html

2. Connotations
   http://leo.stcloudstate.edu/grammar/connotations.html

3. List of Banished Words
   http://www.lssu.edu/banished/current/default.html

Endnotes

1. Source: http://www.geocities.com/CollegePark/6174/jokes/doublespeak.htm
2. From William Lutz, *Beyond Nineteen Eighty-Four*.

PART FIVE

A Weekly Menu of New Words

Most academic disciplines have their own language—a set of specialized words and phrases that have very specific meanings within the field. The following word lists, arranged by academic discipline, will familiarize you with some of the key terminology used in college courses. You will also find these words helpful in everyday life and in the workplace. The first list, Campus Terminology, is intended to help you "speak" the language of college. Here is a list of the disciplines included in this part, along with page references.

SECTION A Campus Terminology

1. **academic dismissal** Withdrawal or denial of enrollment status within the college due to poor grades.

2. **advisor** A faculty member or counselor assigned to help students plan their academic programs.

3. **Articulation agreement** An agreement between a community college and four-year colleges that detail the acceptability of courses in transfer toward meeting specific four-year degree requirements.

4. **certificate** A level of education achieved by the completion of a specified number of courses that prepare students for employment in selected occupational/vocational fields requiring training beyond the high school level.

5. **credit hours** The number of units each course is worth toward completion of degree requirements.

6. **curriculum** The course of study a student pursues to earn a degree.

7. **elective** A course not required for a major field of study or for general education.

8. **general education** A specific group of courses in general academic areas that are required to meet transfer or graduation requirements. General education courses, usually in the arts and sciences, are introductory in nature and teach fundamental knowledge and skills to produce a well-rounded graduate.

9. **GPA (QPA) (Grade Point Average/Quality Point Average)** A system of computing a semester average in which letter grades are assigned a numerical value (A = 4, B = 3, C = 2, D = 1, F = 0). The points corresponding to each letter grade are multiplied by the number of credits for the course, then added up and divided by the total number of credits taken.

10. **lower division/upper division** Courses offered at the freshmen/sophomore level are considered lower division courses. Courses for juniors and seniors are referred to as upper division courses.

11. **major** Series of courses/program of study that leads to a degree. Also refers to the subject area of interest in which a student is pursuing a college degree.

12. **matriculation** Acceptance into a degree-granting program.

13. **pass/fail grade** A grading policy that allows students to earn either a pass grade or a fail grade instead of a letter grade for a particular course.

14. **placement service** A campus office that provides job listings from local or campus employees and assists students in finding full-time jobs after graduation.

15. **prerequisite** A course that must be completed before another can be taken or a competency that must be established before enrollment in a course or program.

16. **professors/academic rank** A system of ranking faculty members, based on their experience, credentials, and teaching skills, as well as research, scholarship, and publications. The lowest ranks are instructor and lecturer. The next highest is assistant professor, followed by associate professor, with the highest rank being full professor. Faculty members, regardless of their rank, are addressed as "professor."

17. **syllabus** (plural: **syllabi**) A course outline that lists course objectives, required reading assignments and due dates, examination dates, and other course requirements such as attendance.

18. **transcript** A copy of a student's academic record that includes semesters attended, courses taken, grades awarded, and units accumulated.

19. **unit** A number that indicates the amount of college credit given for a course and is based on the number of classroom hours of instruction per week. Usually, one unit is equivalent to one lecture hour of class time per week. A course that meets for three lecture hours will usually earn three semester units.

20. **withdrawal, course** A policy that removes a student from an official course or registration; financial or academic penalties may result.

LEARN MORE ABOUT CAMPUS TERMINOLOGY by visiting the following Web site:

http://de.lbcc.edu/terminology.html

EXERCISE 5-1

Supply a word from the list in this section that completes the meaning of each sentence.

1. Samuel earned a _____certificate_____ in horticulture, which prepared him for a position as landscape designer.

2. My psychology course, which met for three hours per week, earned three _____units/credit hours_____.

3. Because Jason had failed all five courses, he was subject to _____academic dismissal_____.

4. When she applied for a part-time job at Sears, Yolanda was asked to submit a copy of her _____transcript_____.

5. To find a part-time job on campus, Sarah visited the _____placement services_____ office.

6. Lia decided to _____major_____ in English because that course of study would prepare her for law school.

7. Introduction to zoology is a four-_____credit hour_____ course.

8. Joshua took several _____general education_____ courses during his first semester; they helped him grasp the breadth of knowledge available in the academic community.

9. Be sure to study each course_____syllabus_____; it will help you know what is expected in each course.

10. Ramona decided to change her _____curriculum_____ from mechanical engineering to liberal arts.

EXERCISE 5-2

Choose the definition in column B that best matches each word or phrase in column A. Write your answer in the space provided.

	Column A		Column B
1. __d__	syllabus	a.	Courses that must be completed before enrollment in other courses or programs
2. __e__	lower division	b.	A faculty member or counselor assigned to help students plan their academic programs
3. __f__	academic dismissal	c.	Series of courses leading to a degree in a particular field
4. __i__	certificate	d.	A course outline that lists course objectives and other course requirements
5. __c__	major	e.	Courses at the freshmen and sophomore level
6. __j__	matriculation	f.	Withdrawal or denial of enrollment status
7. __a__	prerequisites	g.	A system of computing a semester average
8. __b__	advisor	h.	A copy of a student's academic record
9. __g__	GPA (QPA)	i.	Designates completion of courses in preparation for a vocation
10. __h__	transcript	j.	Acceptance into a degree program

Supply a word from the list in this section that completes the meaning of each sentence.

1. Because Julia enjoyed music, she decided to take a history of music course as an
   _____elective_____, although she was not required to do so for her degree in nursing.

2. Because Doug failed the first exam in chemistry and felt lost in the course, he decided to
   submit a _____withdrawal_____ request.

3. Arturio planned to transfer to the University of New Mexico after finishing his degree in business at his nearby community college. He asked if an __articulation agreement__ was in place in the field of business management.

4. Before registering for courses for next semester, Jewel made an appointment with her
   _____advisor_____ to discuss which courses to take as electives.

5. _General education courses_ are designed to acquaint students with knowledge and skill in a wide range of academic disciplines.

6. Because Sam's _____GPA_____ was 4.0, he was eligible for a partial scholarship.

7. Because Franklin knew his math course would be difficult, he elected to take a
   _____pass/fail grade_____ instead of a letter grade that would affect his GPA.

8. In mathematics, be sure to pay attention to course _____prerequisites_____; otherwise, you may find yourself in a course for which you lack background knowledge.

9. Cecelia applied for _____matriculation_____ into the animal management program.

10. A professor's _____academic rank_____ is based on credentials and teaching experience.

SECTION B Computers/Information Systems

1. **cookies** An entry or a file placed on the user's hard drive that stores user profiles. It is often used to personalize a Web site for a frequent visitor.

2. **cyberspace** The Internet and other networks, and the virtual communities they form.

3. **download** To receive and transfer a file electronically from a remote computer.

4. **emoticons (smilees)** Small graphic images produced using keyboard characters that writers substitute for facial expressions. For example, a "smile" is indicated by a colon and a right parenthesis.

5. **GUI (graphical user interface)** An interface that represents programs, files, and options as graphical images instead of text.

6. **hacker** A highly skilled computer user who accesses computer files and systems illegally or without authorization.

7. **homepage** A Web page that functions as an introduction or front door entrance to a Web site.

8. **links (hyperlinks)** A text or image that connects the user to other pages or to other Web sites.

9. **listserv** An ongoing discussion group on a particular topic or issue in which participants subscribe through a central service. Listservs may have a moderator that manages information flow and content.

10. **MIME (Multipurpose Internet Mail Extensions) attachments** A file that is attached to an e-mail message.

11. **multimedia** Software that combines words, graphics, sound, and video.

12. **netiquette** The appropriate behavior expected on the Internet; a combination of the words *Net* (from Internet) and *etiquette.*

13. **network** A computer system that uses communication equipment to connect two or more computers.

14. **RAM (Random Access Memory)** and **ROM (Read Only Memory)** RAM is the computer's electronic memory; it contains data that can be entered into a computer file. ROM is the computer's preprogrammed memory; it can be read but not altered.

15. **search engine** A research tool that allows users to enter keywords to search the Internet for information.

16. **upload** To send a file or application from a local computer to another computer over the Internet.

17. **URL (Uniform Resource Locator)** A string of characters that serves as an address for a file or site on the World Wide Web.

18. **virtual reality (VR)** A system that uses three-dimensional graphics to create an imaginary place that seems very realistic.

19. **virus** An unauthorized program that attaches itself to other computer programs and, after reproducing itself, causes damage or destroys data in those programs.

20. **World Wide Web (WWW)** Part of the Internet containing documents and images connected by hyperlinks.

Note: If you are unfamiliar with computers, be sure to learn the following terms as well: *cursor, data, floppy disk, CD-ROM, mouse, modem, terminal, monitor, hardware, software, CPU, Internet, e-mail.*

LEARN MORE ABOUT COMPUTER-RELATED TERMINOLOGY
by visiting the following Web site:

http://www.instantweb.com/foldoc/index.html

Choose the definition in column B that best matches each word or phrase in column A. Write your answer in the space provided.

	Column A		Column B
1. __d__	listserv	a.	The Internet and other networks, and the virtual communities they form
2. __f__	homepage	b.	A computer system that uses communication equipment to connect two or more computers
3. __e__	download	c.	A computer's electronic preprogrammed memory
4. __h__	MIME attachment	d.	An ongoing discussion group on a particular topic or issue
5. __b__	network	e.	To receive information from another computer
6. __c__	ROM	f.	A Web page that introduces a Web site
7. __j__	virus	g.	A research tool that uses keywords to search for information
8. __g__	search engine	h.	A file attached to an e-mail message
9. __i__	links	i.	Text or an image that leads to other pages or sites
10. __a__	cyberspace	j.	A program that damages or destroys data

EXERCISE 5-5

Supply a word from the list in this section that completes the meaning of each sentence.

1. Because data was missing from her computer, Kyoka wondered if a _____virus_____ had invaded her system.

2. The instructor warned her students to use appropriate _____netiquette_____ when online during class time.

3. The company is trying to find the _____hackers_____ who illegally accessed credit card numbers from its computer files.

4. Abbey realized her computer did not have enough _____RAM_____ when she tried to install her new software program.

5. Because his business was expanding, Jeff decided to use a _____network_____ to connect all the computers in the office.

6. Eva found a _____MIME_____ attached to one of her e-mail messages.

7. The professor told her students they could _____download_____ files from the library Web site.

8. Jeff went to the university's _____homepage_____ to find the academic department's listing.

9. The museum's Web site has many _____ links _____ connecting to all its art galleries and to other museum sites.

10. Because her keywords were not getting enough results, Judith decided to try another _____ search engine _____.

EXERCISE 5-6

Choose the definition in column B that best matches each word or phrase in column A. Write your answer in the space provided.

	Column A		Column B
1. __d__	virtual reality	a.	A text or image that connects to other pages or Web sites
2. __g__	multimedia	b.	To send information from one's own computer to another
3. __c__	World Wide Web	c.	A part of the Internet containing documents and images connected with links
4. __j__	netiquette	d.	A system that uses three-dimensional images to create an imaginary place
5. __a__	links	e.	Graphic images that substitute for facial expressions
6. __f__	cookies	f.	A file that stores data about a computer user's visits to Web sites
7. __h__	hacker	g.	Software that combines words, graphics, sound, and video
8. __i__	URL	h.	A computer user who accesses files without authorization
9. __e__	emoticons	i.	An address for a file or site on the Web
10. __b__	upload	j.	Appropriate behavior expected on the Internet

SECTION C Law

1. **affidavit** A voluntary written statement sworn to before an authorized official.

2. **arraignment** An appearance in court prior to a criminal trial. Often the identity of the defendant is established, the defendant is informed of the charges and of his or her rights, and the defendant is required to enter a plea.

3. **defendant** A person accused of a crime against whom legal action is brought.

4. **deposition** A statement made under oath outside of court that is intended to be used as evidence in court.

5. **entrapment** Improper or illegal encouragement, by law enforcement agents, for a person to commit a crime.

6. **fraud** Intentional deception in order to secure unfair or unlawful gain.

7. **hearsay** Something not based on the personal observations of a witness; it is not usually allowed to be entered as evidence.

8. **indictment** A formal written accusation, submitted to the court by a grand jury, alleging that a certain person has committed a serious crime.

9. **infringement** A violation of a right, law, or contract; wrongful use of a copyright or trade name.

10. **injunction** A court order prohibiting a person from doing a specific act.

11. **jurisdiction** The territory, subject matter, or people over which a court has authority.

12. **lien** The right to take, hold, or sell the property of a debtor as security or payment for a debt.

13. **litigation** Legal proceedings.

14. **misdemeanor** A relatively minor offense punishable by up to one year in jail; an offense less serious than a felony.

15. **plaintiff** A person who initiates or begins a legal action.

16. **plea bargain** To plead guilty to a lesser charge than that of which one is accused; often used in exchange for information or cooperation as a witness by the accused.

17. **proxy** A document in which one person is legally appointed to represent another.

18. **statute** A law enacted by a legislative body.

19. **tort** Damage, injury, or wrongful act done willingly against a person or property for which a civil suit can be brought.

20. **venue** The place where a crime is committed. Also, the geographical area in which a court may hear or try a case.

LEARN MORE ABOUT LEGAL TERMINOLOGY by visiting the following Web site:

http://jurist.law.pitt.edu/dictionary.htm

EXERCISE 5-7

Supply a word from the list in this section that completes the meaning of each sentence.

1. When a police officer improperly encourages a citizen to commit a crime, the officer is guilty of _____entrapment_____ .

2. The abused wife sought an _____injunction_____ to prevent her ex-husband from entering her home.

3. In a trial, the _____plaintiff_____ is the person who initiates the legal action.

4. A statement made under oath outside of court intended to be used as evidence in court is called a _____deposition_____.

5. Mr. Hargrave signed an _____affidavit_____ before a notary stating that he had no knowledge of his son's criminal activities.

6. If you copy several pages of a book and do not give the author credit for the work, you are guilty of copyright _____infringement_____.

7. When Harrison took out a car loan, the finance company placed a _____lien_____ against the car's title.

8. At his _____arraignment_____, Jay, who was accused of car theft, pleaded not guilty.

9. A _____misdemeanor_____ is less serious than a felony and is punishable by up to one year in jail.

10. The president of the corporation was shocked when she received the news of her _____indictment_____ for theft of corporate funds.

EXERCISE 5-8

Choose the definition in column B that best matches each word or phrase in column A. Write your answer in the space provided.

	Column A		Column B
1. __f__	fraud	a.	Something not based on personal observation
2. __e__	statute	b.	Legal proceedings
3. __j__	plea bargain	c.	A voluntary written statement sworn before an authorized official
4. __h__	defendant	d.	A relatively minor offense
5. __i__	venue	e.	A law enacted by a legislative body
6. __d__	misdemeanor	f.	Intentional deception
7. __c__	affidavit	g.	Statement made under oath
8. __a__	hearsay	h.	Person accused of a crime
9. __b__	litigation	i.	Place where a crime is committed
10. __g__	deposition	j.	To plead guilty to a lesser charge

EXERCISE 5-9

Supply a word from the list in this section that completes the meaning of each sentence.

1. In a court case, a person accused of a crime is called the _____defendant_____.

2. In a courtroom, when a witness reports something he or she has not directly experienced, the testimony is known as _____hearsay_____.

3. _____Litigation_____ for consumer fraud cases is expected to take two years.

4. A health care _____proxy_____ allows a person to make medical decisions for another person who is unable to do so.

5. A _____tort_____ refers to a damage or injury for which a civil suit can be brought.

6. A person who deliberately does not report income on his or her federal tax statement is guilty of _____fraud_____ .

7. The man accused of first degree murder agreed to accept a _____plea bargain_____ which reduced the charge to accidental homicide.

8. The defense attorney requested a change of _____venue_____ ; he hoped to move the trial to a district with stronger ethnic representation.

9. The state legislature passed a _____statute_____ making smoking illegal in public buildings.

10. The judge refused to hear the case because it was out of her _____jurisdiction_____ . ▪

SECTION D Health/Medicine

1. **acute** Sudden and requiring immediate treatment, as in *acute appendicitis*.

2. **asymptomatic** Without symptoms.

3. **benign** Nonthreatening, noncancerous, as in a *benign tumor*.

4. **biopsy** The removal of tissue for the purpose of determining the presence of cancerous cells.

5. **contraindications** Conditions suggesting that a drug should not be used.

6. **health care proxy** A legal document that designates another person who can make medical decisions for a person who is unable to direct his or her own care.

7. **holistic** Viewing the body as a whole organism.

8. **HMO (Health Maintenance Organization)** An organization established to provide health care to its members at a fixed price.

9. **idiosyncratic** Unusual or abnormal, as in an *idiosyncratic response* to a drug or food by an individual.

10. **inoculation** The injection or transfer of a substance into the body.

11. **intravenous** Inserting a medication or fluid into the vein using a needle or tube.

12. **living will** A document that specifies the type of care a person does and does not want to receive when his or her death is likely.

13. **malignant** Cancerous.

14. **malpractice** Professional negligence.

15. **noninvasive procedures** Tests or treatments in which the skin and body are not entered.

16. **nurse practitioner (NP)** A registered nurse who has received additional training in an area of specialty, such as obstetrics.

17. **outpatient** Medical treatment that does not require overnight hospital care.

18. **predisposition** The tendency or susceptibility to develop a certain disease or condition.

19. **prognosis** Prediction of the course and outcome of a disease or illness.

20. **rehabilitation** The process of assisting patients to regain a state of health.

WWW

LEARN MORE ABOUT HEALTH-RELATED TERMINOLOGY
by visiting the following Web site:

http://www.mlanet.org/resources/medspeak/index.html

EXERCISE 5-10

Supply a word from the list in this section that completes the meaning of each sentence.

1. The physician advises all of her elderly patients to prepare a _____living will_____ that specifies their wishes for medical care.

2. Arturo had _____acute_____ appendicitis; he was rushed into surgery.

3. The _____biopsy_____ of the tumor on Martha's knee indicated it was not malignant.

4. Because my doctor was unavailable for an immediate appointment, I was given an appointment with the _____nurse practitioner_____.

5. A _____health care proxy_____ allows you to name the person who will make medical decisions for you if you are unable to do so.

6. _____Holistic_____ medicine considers the body as a whole, complete organism.

7. The doctor who operated on his patient's wrong knee was charged with _____malpractice_____.

8. The antibiotic was administered using an _____intravenous_____ needle.

9. The doctor told the patient that his low white blood cell count was _____asymptomatic_____; there were no visible symptoms.

10. Due to the history of heart attacks in his family, Jonathan has a _____predisposition_____ toward heart disease.

EXERCISE 5-11

Write the letter of the correct answer in the space provided.

1. **Acute** refers to
   a. pain in the joints
   b. a sudden injury or illness
   c. muscle spasms
   d. a type of cancer

2. A **living will** specifies

    a. when a person is declared legally deceased

    (c.) the type of care a person wants when his or her death is likely

    b. who can be named in a person's will

    d. the wishes of a diseased person

3. **Prognosis** refers to

    (a.) prediction of the course or outcome of a disease or illness

    c. a medical chart used in hospitals for tracking medications

    b. the type of treatment needed

    d. any procedure using a needle

4. **Asymptomatic** refers to a patient

    a. with symptoms that come and go

    c. in a lot of pain

    b. with only minor pain

    (d.) with no symptoms

5. **Malignant** means

    a. cankerous

    (c.) noncancerous

    b. cancerous

    d. dyspeptic

6. **Outpatient** is a type of medical treatment in which a patient

    a. receives treatment at home

    c. receives treatment at a hospice

    b. requires follow up care after surgery

    (d.) does not stay overnight in a hospital

7. **Contraindications** are conditions which suggest

    a. a disease is spreading

    c. the patient refuses medication

    (b.) a drug should not be used

    d. the wishes of a diseased person

8. **Biopsy** refers to the removal of tissue

    a. in the lungs

    (c.) for determining cancer

    b. for transplant to a recipient

    d. to use for vaccine therapy

9. A **nurse practitioner** is a nurse who

    (a.) has received additional training

    c. does not have a real nursing degree

    b. is only licensed to work in a hospital

    d. is studying to become a midwife

10. **Benign** means

    a. cell growth

    (c.) noncancerous

    b. tumor

    d. abnormal

EXERCISE 5-12

Supply a word from the list in this section that completes the meaning of each sentence.

1. Judith was relieved when she learned the tumor on her wrist was _____benign_____.

2. Many companies provide health care insurance to their employees by enrolling them in an _____HMO_____.

3. My mother's cataract surgery was performed at an _____outpatient_____ surgery center.

4. After surgery, the doctor announced the cancer patient's _____prognosis_____ was good.

5. The patient's response to the chemotherapy was _____idiosyncratic_____; she experienced none of the usual symptoms.

6. After knee replacement surgery, my father needed several weeks of _____rehabilitation_____.

7. The doctor regretfully told his patient that the tumor was _____malignant_____ and that surgery would be necessary.

8. Vision and hearing tests are _____noninvasive_____ procedures.

9. The label on the prescription listed its _____contraindications_____.

10. Everyone exposed to hepatitis should receive an _____inoculation_____.

SECTION E   Education

1. **ability grouping** The arrangement of students into classes based on mastery of specific skills, such as reading or math.

2. **accountability** A policy that requires student progress to be measured and that teachers are responsible for student progress.

3. **bilingual education** An educational program that teaches a second language (often English) to students whose first language is not English and maintains the students' native language as well.

4. **collaborative learning** A learning situation in which students work together on a project or assignment.

5. **competency testing** The measurement of a student's ability to perform a specific skill (such as multiplication) or achieve a specified level (such as reading at a sixth-grade level).

6. **cultural literacy** The familiarity with a body of knowledge that most educated people in a given society share.

7. **curriculum** A course or program of study.

8. **electronic classroom** A learning environment in which students have access to computers, the Internet, and multimedia sources of information.

9. **gifted and talented program** A program of supplemental instruction designed to stimulate and further the growth of students who exhibit high intelligence or exceptional mastery of skills.

10. **home schooling** A policy that allows qualified parents to educate their children at home.

11. **instructional objectives** Specific learning goals or accomplishments that a school or teacher establishes for students. Objectives identify what a student is to learn.

12. **learning community** An environment in which teachers and students come together to provide respect, interaction, and positive feedback in support of students as learners.

13. **literacy** The ability to read and write. Math and computer skills are sometimes considered literacy skills as well.

14. **magnet school** A school that offers special, unique programs to attract students from within a school district.

15. **performance assessment** A form of testing that requires students to show what they know by actually doing something, such as performing a specific task.

16. **phonics** A method of teaching reading that emphasizes letters and the sounds associated with them.

17. **school board** A group of elected officials that serves as a governing body of a school district.

18. **standardized test** A formal, usually commercial test that is administered according to specific directions with time limitations. It is often machine scored; results often compare students' abilities to others in the class, the district, the state, or the nation.

19. **tenure** A policy that allows teachers to hold their positions on a permanent basis without periodic contract renewals.

20. **whole language** A method of teaching that integrates reading, writing, speaking, and listening.

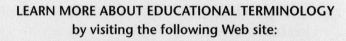

LEARN MORE ABOUT EDUCATIONAL TERMINOLOGY
by visiting the following Web site:

http://vote.learn.unc.edu/glossary/

EXERCISE 5-13

Write the letter of the correct answer in the space provided.

1. **Cultural literacy** refers to:
   a. student improvement
   b. the teaching of values students
   c. familiarity with shared knowledge
   d. the separation of high and low performing

2. **Competency testing** measures students'
   a. skills
   b. attitudes
   c. compatibility
   d. social awareness

3. **Home schooling** occurs when
   a. students study at home
   b. teachers consult with parents at home
   c. students and teachers form communities
   d. parents educate their children at home

4. **Performance assessment** is a form of testing that focuses on
   a. knowing the right answers
   b. thinking critically
   c. reacting to the performance of others
   (d.) carrying out a task

5. A **standardized test** is a
   a. timed oral test
   b. timed essay test
   (c.) timed commercial test
   d. untimed informal test

6. **Whole language**
   (a.) integrates reading, writing, listening, and speaking
   b. focuses on the child as a whole being
   c. emphasizes setting one's own learning objectives
   d. requires students to interact

7. **Collaborative learning** involves
   a. planning an evening of study before beginning
   b. studying by testing yourself
   (c.) working with other students
   d. reviewing the work of others

8. **Ability grouping** is a method of arranging students by
   (a.) skill level
   b. age
   c. social preference
   d. size

9. **Gifted and talented programs** are intended to
   (a.) stimulate further growth of high ability students
   b. help all students work together
   c. separate high and low achieving students
   d. encourage high performing students to take school seriously

10. A **magnet school**
    a. focuses on artistic abilities
    b. focuses on basic skills
    (c.) offers special, unique programs
    d. offers traditional instruction

EXERCISE 5-14

Supply a word from the list in this section that completes the meaning of each sentence.

1. The students were told to work together on a ___collaborative learning___ project to complete the course objectives.

2. Maria chose to ___home school___ her children because she had a degree in early childhood education.

3. The new immigrants were able to benefit from a ___bilingual education___ program for adults at the state university.

4. The voters elected their new ___school board___ members in November.

5. The computers in the ___electronic classroom___ were upgraded last year.

6. The first-grade teacher used ___phonics___ to teach her students how to read.

7. Because the school uses _____ability grouping_____, the students are divided up into several different classes according to skill level.

8. Because Eryn excelled in math and science, the school district decided to place her in a _____gifted and talented program_____.

9. The district has several _____magnet schools_____, that offer special programs in art and music.

10. Keisha wanted to find a university _____curriculum_____ that included liberal arts courses.

EXERCISE 5-15

Write the letter of the correct answer in the space provided.

1. **Tenure** allows teachers to
   a. create their own curriculum
   b. develop individual learning plans for students
   c. hire classroom aides
   d. hold their positions on a permanent basis

2. **Accountability** is a policy that requires that
   a. teachers fail nonperforming students
   b. teachers keep track of their time
   c. students report incidents of cheating
   d. students' progress be measured

3. A **curriculum** is a
   a. list of job opportunities
   b. schedule of tests and exams
   c. collection of required readings
   d. course of study

4. A **learning community** is
   a. a social environment for students
   b. an environment that supports students as learners
   c. a group of students competing for grades
   d. a group of teachers who plan instruction

5. **Phonics** is a method of teaching
   a. mathematics
   b. reading
   c. social studies
   d. science

6. **Bilingual education** is a program that
   a. teaches English to students whose first language is not English
   b. encourages racism among children
   c. teaches a second language to high-ability children
   d. discourages multiculturalism among teachers

7. An **electronic classroom** is a learning environment primarily involving
   a. computer training
   b. computers and other multimedia sources of information
   c. technical job training
   d. reading improvement

8. **Literacy** is the ability to
   a. read and write
   b. work with others
   c. focus one's attention
   d. succeed academically

9. The primary job of a **school board** is to

    (a.) govern the school district

    b. select students

    c. meet with parents

    d. conduct fund-raising campaigns

10. **Instructional objectives** identify

    (a.) what students should learn

    b. how much time is spent on each subject

    c. the methods teachers must use

    d. how grades are to be determined

SECTION F Business

1. **assets** The resources (properties) a firm owns.

2. **audit** An examination of a company's records to check for accuracy.

3. **CEO (chief executive officer)** The person responsible for managing the day-to-day operations of a company and carrying out the policies established by the board of directors.

4. **deflation** A decrease in the level of prices or an increase in purchasing power due to a reduction in available currency and credit.

5. **deficit** Inadequate or insufficient funds; the amount a sum of money falls short of the required amount, as in *a budget deficit.*

6. **dividend** A distribution of earnings to the stockholders of a company.

7. **depreciation** Loss in value due to age, use, or market worth. In accounting, depreciation refers to an allowance made for loss in value of property.

8. **entrepreneur** A person who initiates and assumes the risks of starting a new business.

9. **equity** The remaining value of a business or property once debts and mortgages are subtracted.

10. **fiscal year** A twelve-month period of time in which a business operates and tallies its income and expenses.

11. **franchise** An individually owned business that is associated with a chain of stores and operates under the chain's guidelines.

12. **GNP (gross national product)** The total dollar value of all goods and services produced by all citizens in a country in a given one-year period.

13. **gross income** The total dollar amount of all goods and services sold during a specific period; total income before expenses are deducted.

14. **inflation** A general rise in level of prices or a decline in purchasing power due to the lessening value of the dollar.

15. **liabilities** A firm's debts and financial obligations.

16. **monopoly** An industry in which there is only one company that sells the product or service.

17. **net income** The profit earned by a company or individual after all expenses have been subtracted from total income.

18. **productivity** The average level of output per worker per hour.

19. **recession** Two consecutive three-month periods of decline in a country's gross national product (see GNP).

20. **sole proprietorship** A business that is owned and operated by one person.

LEARN MORE ABOUT BUSINESS TERMINOLOGY by visiting the following Web site:

http://www.usg.edu/galileo/internet/business/bizdict.html

EXERCISE 5-16

Supply a word from the list in this section that completes the meaning of each sentence.

1. If you alone operate a landscaping business, the type of business you own is a _____sole proprietorship_____.

2. A _____fiscal year_____ is the twelve-month period of time in which a business operates.

3. A company's property and inventory are known as its _____assets_____.

4. If you owned a Burger King restaurant, part of a national chain, you would own a _____franchise_____.

5. Several companies offer day care services and wellness centers to improve worker _____productivity_____.

6. Your _____gross income_____ is your total income before expenses are subtracted.

7. A _____recession_____ occurs when there has been a consistent decline in a country's gross national product.

8. If only one company provides garbage disposal in your county, it is a _____monopoly_____.

9. When a company lacks the funds to pay its expenses, a _____deficit_____ occurs.

10. When a new car ages, its loss of value is known as _____depreciation_____.

EXERCISE 5-17

Choose the definition in column B that best matches each word or phrase in column A. Write your answer in the space provided. *Note:* This exercise continues on the next page.

Column A		Column B
1. _g_	fiscal year	a. A distribution of earnings
2. _f_	deflation	b. An individually owned business that is associated with a chain of stores

3.   __i__   liabilities

4.   __j__   sole proprietorship

5.   __c__   assets

6.   __a__   dividend

7.   __h__   inflation

8.   __b__   franchise

9.   __e__   audit

10. __d__   productivity

c. The resources a firm owns

d. Average level of output per worker per hour

e. Examination of a company's records

f. Decrease in level of prices or increase in purchasing power

g. A twelve-month period of time in which a business tallies its income and expenses

h. General rise in level of prices or decline in purchasing power

i. A company's debts and financial obligations

j. A business owned and operated by one person

EXERCISE 5-18

Supply a word from the list in this section that completes the meaning of each sentence.

1. The person responsible for running a company is its _____ CEO _____ .

2. An _____ entrepreneur _____ is a person who initiates or assumes risks in starting a new business.

3. A nation's _____ GNP _____ is the total value of all its goods and services produced during a one-year period.

4. The value of a company once debts and mortgages are subtracted is its _____ equity _____ .

5. When prices fall or purchasing power increases _____ deflation _____ occurs.

6. When products, such as clothing, cost more or you can buy fewer items for the same amount of money, _____ inflation _____ has occurred.

7. A company's debts are known as its _____ liabilities _____ .

8. The distribution of earnings to a company's stockholder is a _____ dividend _____ .

9. An _____ audit _____ of a company may be conducted to discover errors in its financial records.

10. If you owned a carpet cleaning business, your _____ net income _____ would be your profit after you subtracted costs such as equipment, supplies, and insurance. ▮

SECTION G Biology

1. **botany** The scientific study of plant life.

2. **carnivore/herbivore/omnivore** Carnivores are flesh-eating animals; herbivores are animals that feed primarily on plants; omnivores are organisms that consume both plants and animals.

3. **chromosomes** A part of the nucleus of animal and plant cells that carries genes and helps transmit hereditary information.

4. **DNA (deoxyribonucleic acid)** The material of which genes are composed.

5. **fauna/flora** Fauna are the animals of a particular region; flora are the plants of a particular region.

6. **genes** The fundamental hereditary unit, found on chromosomes, that controls the development of hereditary characteristics.

7. **genetics** The branch of biology that studies heredity.

8. **habitat** The natural environment in which a plant or animal lives.

9. **hibernation/estivation** Hibernation refers to passing the winter in a dormant state; estivation refers to spending the summer in a dormant state.

10. **homeostasis** The tendency of an organism to maintain a stable internal environment.

11. **marsupials** Animals such as kangaroos whose newborn live in external pouches where they feed and further develop.

12. **mammals** Warm-blooded vertebrates, including humans, characterized by hair on the skin, and, in the female, milk producing mammary glands.

13. **metabolism** Chemical reactions that involve the synthesis or breakdown of molecules within a living cell.

14. **mutation** A permanent structural change in a DNA molecule that may result in a new trait or characteristic.

15. **natural selection** The theory that the surviving plants and animals of a particular species are those that are strongest and most adaptable.

16. **taxonomy** The classification of organisms into categories or systems based on shared characteristics.

17. **toxin/antitoxin** A toxin is a poisonous substance produced by an organism; an antitoxin is a substance formed in response to a toxin for the purpose of neutralizing it.

18. **transpiration** The loss of water vapor through the membrane or pore of an organism; usually associated with plants during photosynthesis or cooling.

19. **vertebrate/invertebrate** A vertebrate is an animal that has a backbone or spinal column; an invertebrate does not.

20. **zoology** The scientific study of animals.

LEARN MORE ABOUT BIOLOGICAL TERMINOLOGY by visiting the following Web site:

http://biotech.icmb.utexas.edu/pages/dictionary.html

EXERCISE 5-19

Choose the definition in column B that best matches each word or phrase in column A. Write your answer in the space provided.

	Column A		Column B
1. __d__	metabolism	a.	The study of plant life
2. __c__	homeostasis	b.	Flesh-eating animals
3. __h__	gene	c.	The tendency of the body to maintain a stable internal environment
4. __f__	flora	d.	A chemical reaction that involves breakdown of molecules within a cell
5. __e__	mammals	e.	Warm-blooded animals with a spinal column or backbone who nurse their young
6. __a__	botany	f.	The plants of a particular region
7. __i__	transpiration	g.	The study of animals
8. __j__	marsupials	h.	A unit that controls the development of hereditary characteristics
9. __b__	carnivores	i.	The loss of water vapor through a pore or membrane
10. __g__	zoology	j.	Animals whose young live in the mother's external pouch

EXERCISE 5-20

Write the letter of the correct answer in the space provided.

1. **Transpiration** is the loss of water vapor through
   - (a.) the membrane or pore of an organism
   - b. the process of heat transfer
   - c. a phase change between cells of an organism
   - d. the root system

2. **Genetics** is the branch of biology that studies
   - a. reproduction
   - b. plant life
   - (c.) heredity
   - d. mammals

3. A **mutation** is a permanent structural change in
   - (a.) a DNA molecule
   - b. fatty tissue
   - c. the cell wall
   - d. the cell membrane

4. **Natural selection** refers to the theory that species that survive
   - a. adapt and evolve from one basic organism
   - (b.) are strongest and most adaptable
   - c. are more intelligent than other mammals
   - d. have evolved more slowly than other mammals

5. **Botany** is the scientific study of

    a. animals

    b. insects

    (c.) plant life

    d. fish

6. **Zoology** is the scientific study of

    a. plants

    b. zookeeping

    c. sociology of zoos

    (d.) animals

7. **Homeostasis** is

    a. an organism's ability to fight infection or disease

    b. the administration of small doses of a remedy to produce disease-like symptoms

    (c.) an organism's tendency to maintain a stable internal environment

    d. a state of shock to the central nervous system

8. **Metabolism** is the chemical reaction that involves

    a. the change in heart rate through exercise

    (b.) the synthesis of molecules within a living cell

    c. the firing of neurons in brain wave function

    d. the loss of water through perspiration

9. **Carnivores** are animals that

    a. feed primarily on plants

    b. feed on both plants and animals

    c. kill for sport

    (d.) eat flesh

10. **Vertebrates** are animals that

    a. have no backbone or spinal column

    b. live on the ocean floor

    (c.) have a backbone or spinal column

    d. walk upright

EXERCISE 5-21

Choose the definition in column B that best matches each word or phrase in column A. Write your answer in the space provided.

	Column A	Column B
1. __c__	chromosomes	a. The theory that the strongest and most adaptable species survive
2. __j__	genetics	b. Passing the winter in a dormant state
3. __b__	hibernation	c. Parts of the cell nucleus that carry genes
4. __a__	natural selection	d. Animals that lack a spinal column
5. __g__	taxonomy	e. The natural environment in which a plant or animal lives
6. __f__	toxins	f. Poisonous substances
7. __h__	DNA	g. The classification of plants or animals into categories
8. __d__	invertebrates	h. The material of which genes are composed
9. __i__	mutation	i. A change in a molecule that may result in a new trait
10. __e__	habitat	j. The study of heredity

SECTION H Psychology/Sociology

1. **case studies** A type of research that involves close, in-depth observation and analysis of individual people.

2. **cognition** A mental process such as thinking, remembering, and understanding.

3. **culture** A system for living that includes objects, values, and characteristics that people acquire as members of a society.

4. **defense mechanism** A method of reducing anxiety by denying or distorting a situation or problem.

5. **empirical** Refers to information obtained from, or that can be verified by, observation or experimentation.

6. **ethnic group** A collection of people who share a cultural heritage.

7. **ethnocentrism** The belief that one's own culture is superior to that of others.

8. **hypothesis** A tentative explanation about how various events are related to one another that can be tested by further experimentation.

9. **intelligence** The capacity to learn from experience and to adapt to one's environment.

10. **learning** A relatively permanent change in knowledge or behavior that results from experience.

11. **multiculturalism** The study of diverse racial and ethnic groups within a culture.

12. **norms** A social rule that specifies how people should behave.

13. **peer group** A group whose members share the same age or common interests.

14. **reinforcement** A reward or the process of giving a reward after a desirable behavior has occurred.

15. **sanction** A reward for conforming to what is expected or a punishment for violating expectations.

16. **social class** A category of people who have approximately equal income, power, and prestige.

17. **status** One's position in a group or society.

18. **stereotypes** An oversimplified, inaccurate mental picture or conception of others.

19. **value** A socially agreed upon idea about what is good, desirable, or important.

20. **variable** A characteristic that changes from person to person within a population being studied.

LEARN MORE ABOUT SOCIAL SCIENCE TERMINOLOGY
by visiting the following Web site:

http://www.urich.edu/~allison/glossary.html

EXERCISE 5-22

Write the letter of the correct answer in the space provided.

1. A **defense mechanism** is a method of
   a. stimulating non-aggressive behavior
   (b.) denying or distorting a situation
   c. changing behavior
   d. eliminating fear

2. **Learning** results in a change in
   a. brain structure
   b. emotions
   c. group behavior
   (d.) knowledge or behavior

3. **Empirical** evidence can be verified by
   a. comparison with values
   b. identification of perceptions
   (c.) observation or experimentation
   d. analysis of emotions

4. A collection of people who share a cultural heritage is called
   (a.) an ethnic group
   b. a race
   c. a peer group
   d. a reference group

5. The attitude that one's own culture is superior is known as
   a. racism
   b. discrimination
   c. prejudice
   (d.) ethnocentrism

6. **Culture** that includes objects, values, and characteristics can best be described as
   a. an undefined lifestyle
   b. a pattern of economic development
   c. a political structure
   (d.) a system for living

7. Within a population, a **variable** is a characteristic that changes
   (a.) from person to person
   b. from day to day
   c. depending on the researcher
   d. depending on the source

8. If you give a child a candy bar as a reward for cleaning his room especially well, the candy bar is a
   (a.) reinforcement
   b. stereotype
   c. value
   d. variable

9. A **hypothesis** is
   a. a conclusion about behavior
   (b.) an explanation of how events are related
   c. a reason for action
   d. a decision about relationships

10. The capacity to learn from experience and adapt to one's environment is known as
    (a.) intelligence
    b. ethnocentrism
    c. multiculturalism
    d. group interaction

EXERCISE 5-23

Supply a word from the list in this section that completes the meaning of each sentence.

1. A category of people having approximately the same income, power, and prestige is called a _____social class_____ .

2. Information that can be verified from an experiment is considered _____empirical_____ .

3. John's _____peer group_____ shared the same interests in skiing and snowboarding.

4. The researcher conducted detailed _____case studies_____ on ten different families to decide whether her theory about parent-child interactions was worth pursuing.

5. Luis encountered many _____stereotypes_____ about men after he quit his job to stay at home and raise his newborn daughter.

6. A cultural heritage shared by a collection of people is a(n) _____ethnic group_____ .

7. Because Felicia does not agree that schools should offer religious classes, her _____values_____ are different from those of local priests and rabbis.

8. The teacher uses _____reinforcement_____ in her classroom to reward the good behavior of her students.

9. _____Cognition_____ refers to mental processes such as thinking, remembering, or understanding.

10. The social rules that specify how people should behave are called _____norms_____ .

EXERCISE 5-24

Write the letter of the correct answer in the space provided.

1. An oversimplified, inaccurate mental picture or conception of others is referred to as
    (a.) a stereotype
    b. an image
    c. a diversification
    d. a sanction

2. **Cognition** primarily involves
    (a.) thinking and remembering
    b. painting and drawing
    c. swimming
    d. cooking

3. Your position in a group or society is called your
    a. sanction
    b. program
    c. peer group
    (d.) status

4. A **case study** focuses on
    a. a single event
    b. a group
    (c.) an individual person
    d. a problem

5. Having enough money to live comfortably is a commonly agreed upon social

    a. stereotype
           c. sanction

    b. variable
            (d.) value

6. The study of diverse racial and ethnic groups within a culture is known as

    a. environmental studies
      (c.) multiculturalism

    b. ethnocentrism
          d. racial diversity

7. A **norm** is a rule that specifies how people should

    (a.) behave
            c. write

    b. think
             d. communicate

8. A **peer group** shares common

    a. religion
            (c.) age or interests

    b. racial background
      d. housing

9. In society, a punishment for not conforming to what is expected is called a

    (a.) sanction
          c. value

    b. status
           d. norm

10. A category of people who have equal income, power, and prestige is called

    a. an income group
      c. a peer group

    (b.) a social class
       d. a value class

SECTION I   Politics/Government

1. **appropriation** A grant issued in a designated amount of public funds to support a particular project or program.

2. **capitalism** An economic system in which individuals and corporations, not the government, owns businesses.

3. **disenfranchise** To deprive an individual of the right of citizenship, especially the right to vote.

4. **conservative** A person who favors state and local government over the federal government's intervention.

5. **electoral college** An electoral body that officially elects the president and vice president of the United States.

6. **entitlement** A law or policy requiring the government to pay money to people or groups meeting a specific set of conditions or criteria.

7. **expenditures** Federal spending of the money the government receives as revenue (income) from sources such as taxes. Major expenditures are social services and the military.

8. **impeachment** The process of charging a political official with improper conduct while in office.

9. **incumbent** A person who currently holds a political office.

10. **lame duck** An elected official whose power is reduced because he or she has not been reelected to the position or is not allowed to run for the same office again.

11. **left wing** A radical or liberal portion of a group.

12. **liberal** A person who favors governmental action to achieve equal opportunity for all.

13. **lobbying** The process of attempting to persuade or influence the decision making of a government official by someone acting on behalf of a person or group.

14. **pacifism** A belief that opposes war and violence as a means of solving problems or settling disagreements.

15. **patronage** A job, promotion, or contract that is awarded for political reasons rather than merit or competence.

16. **revenues** Financial resources of the government; the income tax is a primary source of revenue.

17. **referendum** A state-level process that gives voters the opportunity to approve or disapprove legislation or a constitutional amendment.

18. **right wing** A conservative portion of a group.

19. **socialism** An economic system in which businesses are owned collectively by the government.

20. **veto** The right of one branch of government to refuse approval of measures proposed by another branch, especially the power of the president to reject a bill proposed by Congress.

LEARN MORE ABOUT POLITICAL SCIENCE/GOVERNMENT TERMINOLOGY
by visiting the following Web site:

http://www.daltonstate.edu/faculty/bguo/p1101/Glossary.htm

EXERCISE 5-25

Choose the definition in column B that best matches each word or phrase in column A. Write your answer in the space provided. *Note:* This exercise continues on the next page.

Column A

1. ___j___ impeachment

2. ___g___ socialism

3. ___a___ left wing

Column B

a. The radical or liberal portion of a group

b. Public funds designated for a specific purpose

c. Awarding a job contract as a political favor

4. __i__ veto

   d. A person who favors governmental action to achieve equality

5. __d__ liberal

   e. To deprive an individual of the right of citizenship

6. __b__ appropriations

   f. A body that officially elects the U.S. president and vice president

7. __h__ lobbying

   g. The system in which the government controls businesses to maintain equality in society

8. __f__ electoral college

   h. The attempt to persuade a government official by an individual or group representative

9. __e__ disenfranchise

   i. The power of the U.S. president to reject a bill proposed by Congress

10. __c__ patronage

   j. The process of charging an elected official with improper conduct

EXERCISE 5-26

Write the letter of the correct answer in the space provided.

1. **Expenditures** refer to
   a. large expense accounts
   b. the national debt
   c. federal surplus from taxes
   d. federal spending of money the government receives

2. **Left wing** is the part of a group that is
   a. conservative
   b. radical or liberal
   c. reserved for Republicans
   d. religious or spiritual

3. **Capitalism** is an economic system in which
   a. individuals and corporations own businesses
   b. corporations and the government own businesses
   c. corporations are taxed at a higher rate than individuals
   d. corporations are given tax breaks

4. **Pacifism** is the belief that
   a. voting is a waste of time
   b. war and violence cannot solve problems
   c. wars have always ended a recession
   d. proper legislation will solve all problems

5. **Veto**, the constitutional power to reject a bill proposed by Congress, can be exercised by the
   a. senate
   b. foreign minister
   c. secretary of state
   d. president

6. **Conservative** refers to a person who
   a. holds a seat in Congress
   b. favors traditional values
   c. favors state and local government
   d. takes no political sides

7. **Electoral college** is a body that officially elects

   (a.) the president and vice-president   c. senators

   b. governors   d. members of the the House of Representatives

8. **Liberal** describes a person who

   a. does not vote   c. is against organized religion

   b. is not tolerant of others   (d.) favors governmental action to achieve equality

9. **Socialism** is an economic system in which

   a. businesses are not taxed   c. each state decides how tax money will be spent

   (b.) businesses are owned collectively by the government   d. groups of states combine their economic resources

10. **Disenfranchise** means to

   (a.) deprive an individual of the right of citizenship   c. close a chain store

   b. allow political prisoners to return to their native countries   d. create government-sponsored funds for businesses

EXERCISE 5-27

Choose the definition in column B that best matches each word or phrase in column A. Write your answer in the space provided.

	Column A		Column B
1. __d__	expenditures	a.	An elected official who has not been, or cannot be, reelected
2. __h__	incumbent	b.	A person who favors state and local governmental control
3. __g__	capitalism	c.	Opposition to war and violence
4. __e__	revenue	d.	Federal spending of money
5. __b__	conservative	e.	Financial resources of the government
6. __c__	pacifism	f.	A process that allows voters to approve or disapprove legislation
7. __a__	lame duck	g.	A system in which individuals and corporations own businesses
8. __f__	referendum	h.	A person who currently holds an elected office
9. __i__	entitlement	i.	A law or policy requiring payment of government funds to specific groups
10. __j__	right wing	j.	Conservative portion of a group

1. **allegory** A story in which characters and/or events stand for abstract ideas or forces, so that the story suggests a deeper symbolic meaning.

2. **anthology** A collection of literary works, often by different authors, combined into a single work.

3. **characterization** The methods an author uses to describe and develop characters in a literary work.

4. **classic** A literary work of the highest quality that has long-lasting value and worth.

5. **criticism, literary** Works written to interpret and evaluate literary works.

6. **denouement** The end of a plot (story) in which the final solution takes place.

7. **expository writing** A type of writing in which the main purpose is to present information.

8. **fiction** A literary work that is imaginative and not factual.

9. **figurative language** Language that makes a comparison between two unlike things that are similar in one particular way. Metaphors and similes are two common types of figurative language.

10. **flashback** A scene in a play or reference in a story that interrupts the story line to show something that has occurred in the past.

11. **genre** A type or category of literature; common genres include prose, poetry, fiction, and drama.

12. **memoir** A narrative or record of events based on personal experience.

13. **mythology** A collection of myths (stories) concerning ancient gods and/or legendary beings.

14. **narrative** A story that relates a series of events, real or imaginary, for the purpose of making a point.

15. **persuasive writing** A type of writing intended to convince readers to accept a particular viewpoint or take a specific action.

16. **plot** The basic story line; the sequence of events and actions through which a story's meaning is expressed.

17. **point of view** The perspective from which a story is told. Two common points of view are first person (I) in which the narrator is telling the story as he or she experiences it, and the third person (he, she, they) in which the story is told as though someone else is experiencing it.

18. **setting** The time, place, and circumstance in which a story occurs.

19. **theme** The central or dominant idea of a story; the main point the author is making about human life or experiences.

20. **tone** How a writer sounds to the reader and how he or she feels about the subject.

EXERCISE 5-28

Supply a word from the list in this section that completes the meaning of each sentence.

1. When Derek wrote his first novel, he wrote from the _____point of view_____ of the first person.

2. The _____setting_____ for Angela's story is the Pacific Northwest.

3. Marianne used _____persuasive writing_____ in her newspaper article to try to convince her readers that the museum needed more money.

4. David studied the gods of ancient Greece in his _____mythology_____ class.

5. The survey course will be using a(n) _____anthology_____ which will cover a collection of poetry from the nineteenth century.

6. Miguel used many _____flashbacks_____ in his short story so that his readers could understand the history of his characters.

7. Because the sequence of events in her story was very confusing, Yolanda wrote an outline of the _____plot_____.

8. The _____tone_____ of Nate's story sounded very angry and hostile to the entire class.

9. A story in which characters or events stand for abstract ideas is called a(n) _____allegory_____.

10. Rosa has decided to write her _____memoirs_____ of her personal experiences in the war.

EXERCISE 5-29

Write the letter of the correct answer in the space provided.

1. setting
   a. time, place and circumstance of a story
   b. events in a story
   c. key people in a story
   d. perspective of a story

2. persuasive writing
   a. writing intended to convince
   b. writing intended to inform
   c. writing intended to discuss
   d. writing intended to express feelings

3. denouement
   a. the end of a story
   b. the action in a story
   c. the introduction to a story
   d. the first event in a story

4. fiction
   a. factual story
   (b.) imaginative story
   c. truthful story
   d. misleading story

5. memoir
   a. story based on interviews
   (b.) record of events based on experience
   c. events that cannot be verified
   d. historical events

6. plot
   a. time period
   b. key people
   c. important idea
   (d.) sequence of events

7. mythology
   a. misleading stories about figures in history
   (b.) stories about ancient gods and goddesses
   c. fictional stories about people
   d. untrue stories about religious figures

8. point of view
   a. actions other characters can view
   b. place where actions occur
   (c.) perspective from which a story is told
   d. point where the story begins

9. narrative
   a. story without a conclusion
   b. story without a theme
   c. story that persuades
   (d.) story that makes a point

10. theme
    a. how the writer sounds
    b. most important character
    (c.) main point of a story
    d. most important event in a story

SECTION K Arts

Music

1. **a capella** Vocal music performed without instrumental accompaniment.

2. **consonance** A combination of sounds considered to be pleasing and harmonious.

3. **dissonance** Disagreeable sounds or those lacking harmony.

4. **ensemble** A musical work performed by two or more musicians or a group of musicians.

5. **maestro** A composer, conductor, or teacher of special importance; master of a particular art.

6. **medley** A musical composition made up of passages selected from different musical works.

7. **rendition** A style or interpretation of a musical piece.

8. **repertoire** A list of musical works a group of musicians is able to perform.

9. **rhythm** A regular pattern of sounds or musical notes created by the variation of the duration and stress of musical notes.

10. **symphony** A musical piece consisting of three or more movements to be played by an orchestra; a large-scale, complex musical piece. Also refers to an orchestra itself.

Visual Arts

1. **aesthetics** The study of the nature, meaning, and expression of beauty, as found in painting, sculpture, and drawing.

2. **collage** A work made by gluing or pasting a variety of materials such as paper, fabric, or photographs on a flat surface.

3. **form** The shape or configuration of an artistic work.

4. **impressionism** A style of painting that is known for short brush strokes to simulate the reflection of light, and for the use of primary colors.

5. **mosaic** An art form in which small squares of marble or other material are laid together to form a pattern or design.

6. **proportion** The relationship between parts with respect to size, quantity, or degree.

7. **realism** A style of painting that intends to show life and objects accurately, as they actually are.

8. **structure** The manner in which the parts of a work are combined.

9. **surrealism** A style of painting that attempts to express the workings of the subconscious mind.

10. **texture** The appearance and feel of the surface of an artistic work.

LEARN MORE ABOUT ART TERMINOLOGY by visiting the following Web site:

http://www.theatrecrafts.com/glossary/glossary.shtml

Choose the definition in column B that best matches each word or phrase in column A. Write your answers in the space provided.

Music

	Column A		Column B
1. __c__	medley	a.	Music sung without instrumental accompaniment
2. __a__	a capella	b.	The regular pattern of sounds created by varying the duration and stress of notes
3. __f__	ensemble	c.	A selection of passages from different musical works
4. __i__	rendition	d.	A musical piece consisting of three or more movements for an orchestra
5. __b__	rhythm	e.	Disagreeable sounds
6. __e__	dissonance	f.	A musical work for two or more musicians
7. __g__	repertoire	g.	The list of works a musician performs
8. __d__	symphony	h.	An important composer or conductor
9. __h__	maestro	i.	The interpretation of a musical piece
10. __j__	consonance	j.	Pleasing and agreeable sounds

Write the letter of the correct answer in the space provided.

1. **Impressionism** is a style of painting that is known for

   a. long brush strokes to create a smooth surface

   b. short brush strokes to simulate reflection and for the use of primary colors

   c. stylistic work that is done very quickly

   d. use of mostly dark colors

2. **Surrealism** attempts to

   a. show only very realistic types of images

   b. encourage the use of primary colors

   c. express the workings of the subconscious mind

   d. create a feeling of immortality for the audience

3. **A capella** is

   a. vocal music performed without instrumental accompaniment

   b. vocal music accompanied by only percussion instruments

   c. a small orchestra

   d. music written for both voice and piano

4. **Dissonance** is

   a. a small distant sound

   (c.) disagreeable sounds or those lacking harmony

   b. a blending of harmonic sound

   d. the cymbals of the drum set

5. **Form** is

   a. the layout of the painting

   c. the type of clay used in sculpture

   (b.) the shape or configuration of an artistic work

   d. stretching the canvas on a frame

6. **Symphony** is a musical piece consisting of

   a. one movement to be played by an orchestra

   c. music for string quartets that is played very slowly

   b. music for three to five instruments

   (d.) three or more movements to be played by an orchestra

7. **Realism** is a style of painting that

   a. was never popular until the twentieth century

   (c.) intends to show life and objects accurately

   b. uses a lot of texture and color

   d. does not show life and objects accurately

8. **Consonance** is a combination of sounds

   a. which are atonal

   c. played by only string instruments

   (b.) considered to be pleasing and harmonious

   d. made up of major thirds and fifths

9. **Medley** refers to a musical work

   a. with one dominant sound or tone

   c. made up of several dominant themes

   (b.) selected from different musical works

   d. by one composer that repeats a specific theme

10. **Collage** is a work made by

   a. using many layers of paint to build a thick surface

   c. adding extra pigment to enhance paint color

   b. using only high gloss paints to create a reflective surface

   (d.) gluing or pasting a variety of materials on a flat surface

Prefixes, Roots, and Suffixes

A Useful Prefixes

Prefix	Meaning	Sample Word
a-	not	asymmetrical
ab-	away	absent
ad-	toward	adhesive
ante/pre-	before	antecedent/premarital
anthropo-	human being	anthropology, anthropomorphic
anti-	against	antiwar
archaeo-	ancient times	archaeology, archaic
bi/di/du-	two	bimonthly/divorce/duet
bio-	life	biology, biotechnology
centi-	hundred	centigrade
circum/peri-	around	circumference/perimeter
com/col/con-	with, together	compile/collide/convene
contra-	against, opposite	contradict
de-	away, from	depart
deci-	ten	decimal
dia-	through	diameter
dis-	part, away, not	disagree
equi-	equal	equidistant
ex/extra-	from, out of, former	ex-wife/extramarital
geo-	earth	geology, geography
gyneco-	woman	gynecology, gynecopathy
hyper-	over, excessive	hyperactive
in/il/ir/im-	not	incorrect/illogical/irreversible/impossible
inter-	between	interpersonal
intro/intra-	within, into, in	introduction
mal-	bad, wrong	malpractice
micro-	small	microscope
milli-	thousand	milligram
mis-	wrongly	misunderstand
mono/uni-	one	monocle/unicycle
multi/poly-	many	multipurpose/polygon
non-	not	nonfiction
peri-	around	perimeter
post-	after	posttest
pseudo-	false	pseudoscientific

Prefix	Meaning	Sample Word
pysch-	mind	psychology, psychopath
quad-	four	quadrant
quint/pent-	five	quintet/pentagon
re-	back, again	review
retro-	backward	retrospect
semi-	half	semicircle
sub-	under, below	submarine
super-	above, extra	supercharge
tele-	far	telescope
theo-	God or gods	theology, theologian
trans-	across, over	transcontinental
tri-	three	triangle
un-	not	unpopular

B. Useful Roots

Root	Meaning	Example
am	love	amorous
ann	year	annual
aster/astro	star	asteroid, astronaut
aud/audit	hear	audible, audition
bene	good, well	benefit
bio	life	biology
cap	take, hold	capacity
cede	go	exceed
chron(o)	time	chronology
cord	heart	cordial
corp	body	corpse
cred	believe	credible
cur	run	excursion
dent	tooth	dentist
dict	tell, say	dictionary
duc/duct	lead	introduce
fact/fac	make, do	factory
fid	trust	confident
form	shape	transform
geo	earth	geophysics
graph	write	telegraph
ject	throw	reject
lab	work	laborer
liber	free	liberty
log/logo/logy	study, thought	psychology
loqu	speak	colloquial
lust	shine	luster
man	hand	manual
mis/mit	send	missile
mort/mor	die, death	immortal
nat	born	native
path	feeling	sympathy
ped	foot	podiatrist
pel	drive	propel
phono	sound, voice	telephone
photo	light	photosensitive
pop	people	populace
port	carry	portable
rupt	break	interrupt
scrib/script	write	inscription
sect	cut	intersection

Root	Meaning	Example
sen	feel	sensitive
sen/sent	feel	insensitive
spec	look	spectator
sym/syn	same	synonym
tend/tent/tens	stretch or strain	tension
terr/terre	land, earth	territory
theo	god	theology
tract	pull	attraction
vac	empty	vacant
ven/vent	come	convention
ver	turn	inversion
vert/vers	turn	invert
vis/vid	see	invisible/video
voc	call	vocation

C Useful Suffixes

Suffix	Sample Word
Suffixes that refer to a state, condition, or quality	
-able	touchable
-ance	assistance
-ation	confrontation
-ence	reference
-ible	tangible
-ion	discussion
-ity	superiority
-ive	permissive
-ment	amazement
-ness	kindness
-ous	jealous
-ty	loyalty
-y	creamy
Suffixes that mean "one who"	
-an	Italian
-ant	participant
-ee	referee
-eer	engineer
-ent	resident
-er	teacher
-ist	activist
-or	advisor
Suffixes that mean "pertaining to or referring to"	
-al	autumnal
-hood	brotherhood
-ship	friendship
-ward	homeward
Suffixes Used to Form Verbs	
-ate	motivate
-ify	quantify
-ize	customize
Suffix Used to Form Adverbs	
-ly	lively
-able, -ible	touchable
-ac, -ic	psychic
-al	minimal
-ant	belligerent
-ary	contrary
-dom	freedom

Suffix	Sample Word

Suffixes Used to Form Adjectives

-en	brazen
-ful	faithful
-ive	attentive
-like	birdlike
-ous, -ious	anxious
-some	wholesome
-y	cloudy

Suffixes Used to Form Nouns

-ac	insomniac
-ance, -ancy	pregnancy
-ary	adversary
-dom	kingdom
-ence	independence
-er	teacher
-hood	parenthood
-ion, -tion	transaction
-ism	tourism
-ist	activist
-ment	employment
-ness	kindness
-ship	friendship
-ure	tenure

ACKNOWLEDGMENTS

Text

Pages 4–15: Pronunciation key and entries for "dismount," "dismiss," "familiar," "found1," "found2," and "oblique." Copyright © 2000 by Houghton Mifflin Company. Reproduced by permission from *The American Heritage Dictionary of the English Language,* Fourth Edition.

Page 16: From *Roget's 21st Century Thesaurus.* Copyright © 1992, 1993, 1999, 2005 by The Philip Lief Group. Published by Dell Publishing. Reprinted by permission of The Philip Lief Group.

Page 22: From Merriam-Webster Online at www.Merriam-Webster.com. Copyright © 2004 Merriam-Webster, Inc. By permission.

Page 23: Adapted from Campbell, Mitchell, and Reece, *Biology: Concepts and Connections,* Third Edition, p. 432. Copyright © 2000. Reprinted by permission of Pearson Education, Inc.

Page 42: John A. Garraty and Mark C. Carnes, *The American Nation,* Tenth Edition, p. 267. New York: Longman, 2000.

Page 43: Adapted from Campbell, Mitchell, and Reece, *Biology: Concepts and Connections,* Third Edition, p. 1. Copyright © 2000. Reprinted by permission of Pearson Education, Inc.

Page 44: Joe L. Kincheloe, Patrick Slattery, and Shirley R. Steinberg, *Contextualizing Teaching,* pp. 68–69. New York: Longman, 2000.

Page 58: James M. Henslin, *Social Problems,* Sixth Edition, pp. 72, 118. © 2003. Reprinted by permission of Pearson Education, Inc., Upper Saddle River, NJ.

Page 58: Michael D. Johnson, *Human Biology: Concepts and Current Issues,* Second Edition, p. 27. San Francisco: Benjamin/Cummings, 2003.

Page 59: "Mnemonics Cartoons—BIO" from www.geocities.com/spenoff reprinted by permission of Ernest Spencer. Copyright © 1999 by Ernest Spencer.

Page 61: ROOTONYMS®, a Rooty*Hoot*Hoot*® Brand Word Puzzle and Answers by Jan and Carey Orr Cook. Reprinted by permission of Carey Orr Cook, Vocabulary University®. http://www.vocabulary.com.

Pages 69, 70: Edward F. Bergman and William H. Renwick, *Introduction to Geography,* Second Edition, pp. 323, 329, 332. Upper Saddle River, NJ: Prentice Hall, 2002.

Page 76: James M. Henslin, *Social Problems,* Sixth Edition, pp. 187, 192, 205. © 2003. Reprinted by permission of Pearson Education, Inc. Upper Saddle River, NJ.

Page 77: Philip G. Zimbardo and Richard J. Gerrig, *Psychology and Life,* 15th Edition, pp. 404–405. New York: Longman, 1999.

Page 78: Adapted from Steven A. Beebe and John T. Masterson, *Communicating in Small Groups,* Sixth Edition, pp. 120–122. Copyright © 2000 by Addison Wesley Longman. Reprinted by permission of Allyn and Bacon, a division of Pearson Education, Inc.

Page 79: Adapted from Campbell, Mitchell, and Reece, *Biology: Concepts and Connections,* Third Edition, p. 593. Copyright © 2000. Reprinted by permission of Pearson Education, Inc.

Photo

Page 2: PM Images / Stone / Getty Images; **9:** © 2005 Randy Glasbergen. Reprinted with permission from www.glasbergen.com; **16:** Terry Warner/www.CartoonStock.com; **26:** Elmer.Parolini/www.CatoonStock.com; **38 (left):** Hulton Archive / Getty Images; **38 (right):** Burke / Triolo Productions / Brand X Pictures / Getty Images; **105:** © Bonnie Kamin/Photo Edit. All rights reserved.

INDEX